Swimming
Up the Sun

Nicole J. Burton

Swimming Up the Sun

A Memoir of Adoption

Nicole J. Burton

APC

Apippa Publishing Company

Riverdale Park, Maryland

First edition.

Visit NicoleJBurton.com for additional news and information.

Library of Congress Control Number: 2007908836
Burton, Nicole J.

Swimming Up the Sun: A Memoir of Adoption/Nicole J. Burton. 1st ed.

ISBN: 978-0-9798992-0-1

1. Memoir   2. Adoption   3. Jewish Studies

ATTENTION CORPORATIONS, UNIVERSITIES, COLLEGES, AND PROFESSIONAL ORGANIZATIONS: Quantity discounts are available on bulk purchases of this book for educational purposes, fundraising, or gift-giving. Contact APC, P.O. Box 54, Riverdale Park, MD 20738.

Manufactured in the United States of America.

For adopted people everywhere

For . . . I have been a stranger
in a strange land.

Exodus 2:22

To swim up the sun, *v.* —*intr.* [*colloq.* British English]

To swim toward the rising sun along a glimmering carpet of stars; to go forth adventurously, usually alone; to swim away from shore toward the unknown . . .

Acknowledgments

In 1989, I joined Toastmasters International and, for my ice-breaker speech, I told this story as I knew it up to that time. I owe a debt of thanks to my fellow Toastmasters for encouraging me to extend the ten-minute speech into a book.

Gracious thanks to my writer friends for their thoughtful reading and encouragement: Terryl Paiste, Grady Smith, Garland Standrod, Grace Topping, and Beth Joselow.

To my extended family, "Angela" and the "Saddler" family, Roger and Peggy Burton, Rebecca Minson and Averill Minson, Rochelle Madill, and Danny and Eileen Rubins; to the memory of my beloved parents, Jean (Moo) Pannizut, "Eve Saddler," and Philip Minson.

To the many helpers along the way, especially Gail Winston, Joann Malone, Jeanine Cogan, and Roland Walker; to my adoption search brothers and sisters in the Adoptee-Birthparent Support

Network and the NORCAP organization; and to the late Norah Reap for her inspiring story of Jewish homecoming.

And to my husband Jim Landry for his limitless faith and encouragement.

Chapter 1

I n 1978, I flew eastward into the velvet darkness to England. In my handbag was an appointment letter to meet the man who would grant me a birth certificate. My adoption search had been an on-again off-again affair, reflecting my ambivalence as well as the obstacle of distance, but a month after I'd read about the change in British adoption law, the letter in the official brown envelope had arrived at my home in Washington, D.C., confirming my request for a counseling appointment.

I possessed a copy of my adoption order but I'd never seen my birth certificate. Now at the age of 21, I would be allowed to. The flight attendant passed by with a tray of miniature cordials, and as we sped through the night in a slim metal tube, I toasted my reflection in the window.

I had always wanted to know my birth parents. I'd felt them calling through the years of childhood. Not because I'd been particularly unhappy. My childhood wasn't perfect but there had been love, a brother and sister, good schools, travel, books, and the pantomime at Christmas. Wanting to find my birth parents had less to do with my childhood and more to do with yearning to learn the shapes of their faces, the gestures of their hands, and the geography of their hearts.

Illuminated in a pool of light amid the dark cabin, I reread the letter with shaking hands, but I never entertained any possibility but the search. I had no real doubts. From the time I could remember my own name, before I could possibly reason out the implications, the knowledge that I would one day search for and find my parents had been a constant companion.

In the artificial dawn of the immigration hall, a man in a navy blue uniform stamped my American passport and murmured a minimal welcome. I waited with the other sleep-deprived travelers for the luggage conveyer to disgorge our bags. I knew more about myself than many adoptees did, that my mother had been a young British artist and my father the son of a Jewish haberdasher in the midlands city of Nottingham. I'd been told they couldn't marry because of religion, that his parents would never have accepted a non-Jewish girl. I knew her name was Eve.* It appeared on the adoption order.

A young Indian woman in a golden sari nuzzled her strapping Nordic husband as we waited for our luggage. How times had changed. Growing up in England knowing I was half-Jewish, I had sensed that being Jewish carried a scent of foreignness; that I was from a different race as well as religion. It was a scent some people begrudgingly admired but others resented. I heard a lot about the war as a child, about Hitler, and the Nazis. I recall when *Life* magazine ran a commemorative photo essay on the concentration camps. When I asked Moo, my adoptive mother, about the Jews, she bought me a copy of *The Diary of Anne Frank*

*At my mother's request, her name and those of her family are changed.

and left me to work it out for myself. Since I'd never met any other Jews, I wondered if I could possibly be the last one left. Yet I knew in my bones that my real father was out there somewhere. Knowing nothing about Jewish religion or culture, I gleaned that being Jewish was both dangerous and special.

I had brought only a small, soft-sided bag, which carried all I needed with room to spare. It was a treat to buy a few new clothes when I came to England; they were like touchstones: a wooly from Marks and Sparks, something cheap and cheerful from Dottie Perkins, perhaps a silk scarf splurge in the West End. We'd immigrated to the States at the end of the 1960s and I hadn't returned often. When I did travel here, I was nostalgic for the tastes and sights of the old days. This visit was to be more about the present and, who knew, perhaps the future. As my bus jogged through the snarl of London morning traffic, a chasm of expectation opened. Who would I find? What would they be like? Would they like me? It wasn't too late to cancel the appointment. It wasn't too late to halt this vehicle propelling me forward and backward. It wasn't too late to stop, go sightseeing instead, or prowl the markets.

The summer rain spat sideways against the bus window, distorting the view. I would not cancel my appointment; I couldn't stand not knowing anymore. When the stop came, I grabbed my bag from the luggage shelf and disembarked. My search had begun.

Chapter 2

I flipped nervously through a *Vogue* magazine in Room 220 of the London General Register Office. Two other women sat in the waiting area. Were they also adopted? Except for my adopted sister, I'd never met any others. I thought about the adoption order tucked in my bag and had no idea what to expect. Perhaps a red silk curtain would be drawn aside and my birth mother would be waiting with arms outstretched and she would say, "I'm *so* happy to see you." Perhaps tears would course down her soft cheeks. Perhaps she would squeeze me tight and her perfume would be *Tabu*. To the secretary behind the desk, the three of us appeared calm as we dutifully paged through our magazines, but to me, the waiting room was peopled with ecstatic, ghostly reunions.

The counselor's hand was cool and dry when he shook mine. Mr. C.E. Day welcomed me into his cramped office and sat next to me in a visitor chair.

"Now, before I grant you your birth certificate, I'd like to ask you a few questions. Don't be concerned, it's rather a formality." I was immediately very concerned. "Why do you want to trace your birth mother?"

I couldn't speak for fear of giving the wrong answer. Was she in the file folders on his desk? I mustered a steady voice and said, "I've always wanted to know who she is."

"Of course," he said, gently. He seemed pleasant. Surely he wouldn't fail me. I was, after all, a naturally good test-taker. "About your adoptive family. You have a brother and sister I see. Did you have a good upbringing? Given the ups and downs of any family, of course."

If my mother had been Lizzie Borden herself and my father Jack the Ripper, I would have replied the same: "Very nice. We were a happy family."

"I see you live in the States now. How do you like the States?" What was he getting at? Was I wrong to leave? Could he deny me my papers for not being an English resident?

"I like America," I said, "but I miss England and come back to visit."

"Right then." He reached over and lifted a folder from the worn wooden desk. I glimpsed my own letter requesting an appointment and my application. He handed me an orange and brown brochure entitled *Access to birth records—Information for adopted people*. Its highlights were printed in orange ink:

~ The new legal rights of adopted persons over eighteen
~ The purpose of counseling
~ How to apply
~ Places where you can meet a counselor
~ Where to send your application form
~ Overseas applicants
~ Meeting the counselor
~ What the counselor can tell you

~ Birth records

~ Further information

"May I see your adoption papers?" He studied them and referred to information in the file. "There's not much new I can add to what you already know. Unfortunately, your father's name doesn't appear on the birth certificate. There are many reasons why that happened. For one thing, the registrar requires proof of the father. He would have had to be present at the registration, and that only happens in one out of a hundred cases." I jotted down what he said because I knew I wouldn't remember everything.

"The address of your mother on the birth certificate may be the address of a nursing home or it may be her home address at the time."

My mother. He hadn't shown me the birth certificate yet. He was just reading from the file. "May I see my birth certificate?" I asked.

"I don't have a copy of it here. You'll have to request it at the records office downstairs, and they'll mail it to you. It shouldn't take very long. If and when you locate your birth mother, you should think very carefully about how to approach her." He pointed to the last section in the brochure, "Further information."

"As you can see here, your adoption agency may have more information." He checked the file again. "You were adopted through the Ledbury Court, which comes under the Gloucester County Services Council, but you were registered in Nottingham. Gloucester's quite good. I'll give you their number. One of their probation officers would have prepared something called the Guardian Ad Litem. It's a confidential report made as a recommendation to the Court. In your case, it would have been filed with Gloucester Social Services. Sometimes it contains useful information. They'll be able to give you the name of the adoption agency in Nottingham as well." He signed a form and handed it to me. It was my birth certificate application form. He smiled. "That wasn't too bad, was it?" I smiled back and took the form. "When you think you're close to finding her, give me a call," he added. He handed me his telephone number and the number of the Gloucester Council on a slip of paper.

"We can try to have a third party make the initial contact for you. A caseworker would visit the family and make a report of the current situation. Saves everyone's feelings that way." Everyone's feelings? It would be a magical caseworker indeed who could spare everyone's feelings in adoption. No red silk curtain but an approved application. I had passed Obstacle One—The Counselor. "Good luck, and do let me know how you get on." When he shook my hand again, it felt warmer.

Downstairs at the cashier's window, I paid about $5.00 for my birth certificate, twice as much as the government adoption fee my father had paid for me, according to my adoption order. Inflation. In the adjacent room, a dozen people searched in huge black leather bound books marked "Births," "Deaths," and "Marriages." I looked myself up for the first time, finding an entry that said "July 25, 1956, Nottingham, Nottinghamshire, Pippa Wright. Mother: Eve Langston Wright."

There I am, I thought. There she is, and there we are together! I stood at the fork of knowing and not knowing, and as I re-shelved the heavy leather volume, I was grinning. Under the yellow and white striped awning of the outdoor café next door, I sipped espresso amid the fumes of central London. The reality of being an adult adoptee was that officials were kind but treated us like wards of the state. We needed approval from strangers to get the information other adults milling around would take for granted, and we were, above all, expected to behave ourselves like fortunate and obedient children, hands in our laps, pinkies raised over china cups, reporting to counselors, saving everyone's feelings. There it was again. No problem. Years of acting uninterested in my own history had prepared me perfectly for passing in the non-adopted world. Inside I was a she-warrior with a lion heart; I would follow every lead until it died.

I didn't think I'd learned much that was new during the interview, but when my birth certificate arrived in the States, I would at least have an address for Eve, albeit one that was over twenty years old. In the meantime, armed with the slip of blue paper given me by Mr. Day, I decided to visit Nottingham to search out my adoption agency. I liked how that sounded, *my adoption agency*. I caught the Underground train to my girlfriend Fiona's apartment in Whitten. All the way through grimy tunnels and stations, imperceptible to the other passengers, I took soundings from my beating heart and stroked steadily out to sea, straight into the current.

Waiting for me at the bus station in Nottingham, smiling through her slightly bucked teeth, was my Auntie Gerrie. She wasn't a real aunt but an old friend of my adoptive mother's. My adoptive parents, Roger and Jean Burton, had recently divorced and "Moo," as I called my adoptive mother, was now living in Italy with her new husband. My father Roger had been an officer in the Royal Air Force, but throughout our family's frequent relocations, Gerrie and Moo had corresponded, and Gerrie had visited us often. I liked her; she was Canadian, as friendly and down-to-earth as an American. She'd been a WAF in the Canadian Women's Air Force during the war, and she and Moo had both been secretaries at the University of Nottingham before Moo married my father. Gerrie herself had never married. She delighted in her friends' children, and I'd always loved her adult attention. She had told me about her trips to Spain, brought her oil paints with her on vacation, and when she took up color photography, explained passionately how she had begun dreaming in Technicolor. When I'd phoned her from London, she immediately offered me a place to stay while I searched in Nottingham. I stepped off the bus into her arms, and she carried my bag to the car, quizzing me as we drove to Sherwood. "What did you find out in London?"

"I called Gloucester Social Services and got the name of my adoption agency, the Catholic Children's Society in West Bridgeford. Is that far?" I said.

"West Bridgeford's not far. I can run you over there," she said. "You'd better call them first." I told her I'd try to set something up for the next day. This was my first visit ever to Nottingham. Moo used to weave stories about the magical midsummer nights at Nottingham's Goose Fair. Standing at her elbow in the kitchen, I would stir the white sauce as she grated the cheese, and she'd tell stories of how she and her mother had baked cakes without milk or eggs or butter during wartime. How they'd blacked out their windows with dark sheets every night to protect themselves from the German bombers roaring overhead into the heart of the Midlands. How she hadn't seen an orange for ten years. Nottingham was where Moo grew up, where it all happened for her. As we crossed a bridge over a skein of railway tracks, I saw clots of factories lying off in the distance to the east and beyond them, the great River Trent. Nottingham was larger and more industrial than I'd imagined from Moo's stories.

Instead of going through the city center, Gerrie drove us up the gentle hills to the suburb of Sherwood. We passed rows of mock Tudor houses. They were semi-detached, built of russet brick and fronted with black tarred beams and white stucco, each with a tidy English flower garden in full bloom. With their barrel chested bay windows, they looked as sturdy as medieval merchants. It always astounded me how English flowers could bloom as they did in the overcast and chilly summers of my childhood. After a stretch of silence, Gerrie remarked that she didn't remember my birth mother being Catholic. I said I didn't either, and we pondered this together.

After we arrived at her house, I called the Catholic Children's Society. A recording told me the number had been changed, and when I called the new number, the receptionist answered, "Southwell Diocesan Society." According to the receptionist, the Catholic Children's Society had gone out of business years ago, and their records had been assumed by another adoption agency. When I was connected to the senior caseworker, I explained I was in search of information. She took down my particulars, and we arranged to meet the next day.

After dinner and television, Gerrie made me comfortable in her cold guestroom. I'd forgotten August was not really a summer month in England, as I had come to think of summer in Washington, roaming carefree in shorts and sandals. Gerrie lent me a flannel nightgown and beneath a paisley feather comforter I snuggled in to the sound of rain slashing at the windows again. What would I find tomorrow? I wondered. Would there be a letter from Eve in my file, asking me to get in touch right away? Such things were known to happen, I'd read about them in my British adoptee newsletter. Perhaps by tomorrow evening, we'd be having tea together at The Copper Kettle. Perhaps she'd be young and beautiful and reach out to me? Perhaps, perhaps . . . the jaws of sleep closed tightly around me.

Mrs. Hall, the adoption officer, was waiting for me at the Southwell Diocesan Society. She had both good and bad news. "Unfortunately, many of the Catholic Children's Society records from 1956 and before were damaged by water in the 1960s. The file on your birth mother and most of the files on the adoptees are gone. Destroyed. I'm sorry."

The only records anyone had on my adoption were lost? Why hadn't they been more careful? Why had I never heard of this happening before? Who was trying to keep information from me? My thoughts lurched and raced, but Mrs. Hall continued steadily. "I did manage to find some information showing you definitely were adopted through the agency. Would you like a cup of tea while we talk? I'm sure you would." Yes, please, a cup of tea, the English panacea for soothing shocks and smoothing life's jolts and pains, and it worked.

We sat in her office, drinking milky tea. I was reeling from the specter of my papers—my beloved documents—possibly even my own mother's letter, swirling down a gigantic black drain, sucked into a slimy sewer along with the records of all the other poor pre-1956 adoptees, down to the bottom of a violent, impenetrable sea. Mrs. Hall placed a yellowed index card in my hand. It read "Eve Wright." "This was our system before office automation," she said, smiling. "Of course, you know your mother's name already." Had Eve touched this card? Was this as far as my search would lead?

Mrs. Hall had done some research and began reading from handwritten notes on a pad of lined white paper. "Dr. Grove was the adoption officer in 1956. She's in her seventies now, lives in Cambridge. She handled cases for twenty four children in 1956, of which twelve resulted in adoptions made in 1956. The others would be listed later. Of those twelve, eight files have been misplaced, including yours." I must have looked bereft because in the next moment, she reached over and placed her hand on my arm. I glanced down at her golden wedding ring and her diamond solitaire. How could she understand? "Even if the file were here, we might not have anything," she said, quietly. "Today, we take down so much more information. You've applied for your birth certificate, haven't you?" I nodded, unable to speak. "Good. I can tell you a few more things, based on the monthly log book, which luckily did survive."

Startled, I looked at her. She had something to give me after all. "You were born at the Nottingham City Hospital on July 25, 1956. The next day, you went to Balmoral Nursing Home, where you stayed from July 26 to August 11—with your mother. You were collected from the Hollies, 8 Maperley Road, on August 25. That was your date of placement." She turned over the page and continued reading. "The Hollies was a mother and baby home, run by the town authority. However, my records show your mother was not at the Hollies; you were there alone."

I scrawled everything on the back of an envelope; I didn't want to forget a single detail. I was still swirling like a torn leaf down the drain of lost records. August 11, the day that she relinquished me; August 11, today's date. While I listened and wrote, questions rose in my mind like bubbles breaking on the surface of a pond. Did we really spend two weeks together at a nursing home? When did she decide to give me up?

Mrs. Hall nibbled her pen. "I wonder why your adoptive parents didn't apply in Herefordshire, near where they lived?" I explained that my adoptive mother was from Nottingham, and how Mr. Day thought I might be able to obtain the court's Guardian Ad Litem report. Mrs. Hall shook her head. "The report was probably destroyed," she said. "They aren't usually kept."

More papers gone. It was infuriating how non-adopted people so casually disposed of our records. Didn't they understand that was all we had? Mrs. Hall continued, " . . . went through Hereford Court, not Nottingham. I have to tell you, that's unusual. I wonder if someone intervened." She reviewed her notes.

"There was money in the family. At least, someone paid for a nursing home for two weeks for you and your mother. Your father, perhaps? That didn't happen often. Eve was only at the hospital for twenty-four hours. She was twenty-three, did you know that?" This was new information. When she had me, she was only about a year older than I was now, a young woman, but not a teenager.

"Ah, here's something else. Yes! I see. She was not known to the agency until July 31st, 1956. That's when she was referred to us." Mrs. Hall looked up at me. "That was a week after you were born."

"What does that mean?"

"I can't be positive, but I would guess you were a concealed pregnancy. Usually, young women made arrangements before the birth, but sometimes, they tried to keep their pregnancies secret as long as they could. Then they didn't contact us until after the birth, when the hospital referred them. I can't be sure, but the late date is a strong indication that's what happened," she said. A concealed pregnancy. I was a secret baby? "I don't know if the agency made home visits to your adoptive parents in Colwall. It was a bit far, but usually they would."

She examined my adoption order. "December 13th. It took almost four months to get the adoption order. That's about right. The law requires that a child be six weeks old before the application is made." I thought but didn't dare ask: Was that to give Eve a chance to change her mind? Did she wait two weeks before deciding to give me up because she was uncertain about what to do? If my father had given her money, perhaps there was some other reason. If he had given her money, why didn't he do more? Why didn't he marry her? The taboo against asking questions made it impossible for me to speak my mind, even to Mrs. Hall.

"Do you know anything about your father?" she asked. I told her that my adoptive mother said that his family ran a haberdashery in Nottingham and that they were Jewish. "The only haberdashery I can think of now is Roughton's on Derby Road. They've been around as long as I can remember. I don't know if they're Jewish, though." More new information; I wrote it all down. This frankness with which she spoke to me and made suggestions, this was new too. My parents had prided themselves on their open-mindedness, but adoption was a loaded gun. My attempts to pry out information were cautiously worded and carefully planned. I sensed from them that they'd be injured if I showed too much interest. I knew without being told that a child who'd been put up for adoption had to be careful; she could be returned to an orphanage or children's home. Yet here was a woman, a social worker, talking as if an adoptee's history were the most open subject in the world. I shivered with a silvery thrill at my new recklessness.

"What are you planning to do next?" Mrs. Hall asked as we stood up to leave.

"I'm going to talk to Canon Ingles at St. Peter's Church," I said. "He married my adoptive parents and was a family friend. My mother once told me his wife sat on my adoption board," I said.

"Good," she said. Then she looked straight at me and her soft gray eyes turned to steel for an instant. "Let me offer a word of advice, if I may. Some of us, such as myself and most of the staff here, feel it's perfectly normal for adoptees to be curious about their birth families, and yes, even search. But there's another school of thought that says you should leave it alone. If you meet someone like that from the Old School, do remember they mean well, but don't pay much attention to what they *say*. I understand why you have to search." She took my hand in hers and shook it. "I understand very well. Good luck!" When later I encountered Canon Ingles, I appreciated Mrs. Hall's warning and her encouragement.

Canon Ingles was pleased to see me, having known Moo and her family for many years. When my grandfather died, according to Moo, the well-wishers at the funeral service spilled out of the doors of St. Peter's Church into the surrounding cobblestone square. An old gentleman in black church robes, Canon Ingles moved with the staccato vigor of a wind-up toy. He appeared intelligent and kind.

I had told him on the phone why I was calling, and he showed no displeasure that I was after adoption information. In fact, he invited me to tea and proudly showed me around the little stone church, pointing out the latest stained glass window and brass fittings. Then we walked over to the rectory, where he asked after my mother and life in America and spoke fondly of Moo's father, my grandfather. Thinking the old dear had forgotten the acknowledged reason for my visit, I eventually asked him directly. "Did you know my birth mother?" Moo had hinted that he knew her family as well.

Canon Ingles paused and smiled, as if contemplating his new window. "Oh, dear," he said, finally. "That was so long ago. I'm afraid I don't remember a thing." The pit of my stomach churned; I sensed he was being cagey and pressed him whether he actually knew her family. "Heavens! What gave you that idea?" he said, all round-eyed innocence beneath his shining, bald head. Now I knew he was lying. He actually clapped his hands together and gazed up at the ceiling. I was suddenly face to face with a cartoon of Friar Tuck. I told him Moo had said he knew both the families.

"Did she, now?" he answered and rearranged his vestments, still smiling with absurd liturgical sweetness. We sat silently in the chilly rectory. This was why I'd come to see him, I reminded myself. Not to have tea or look at the church windows; I'd been forthcoming about my mission. I had no intention of leaving without finding out all I could. I could hear birds singing outside in the churchyard. Finally, he shuffled his feet, and when he looked at me again, his face was sour and he was evidently annoyed. I'd put him on the spot but I had warned him. Mrs. Hall's visit had made me bolder. She'd given me confidence in my search.

"I met your mother's family once," he admitted. He was sitting behind a wooden desk strewn with hundreds of papers and bills. The shelves were filled with moldering leather-bound books. Then he smiled, and I thought he'd remembered something. I poised my pen.

"Yes," he said, "Your mother was married within a few months of the adoption. My wife was a member of the adoption committee. She wasn't a Nottingham girl, no, no. She'd been to school in the area, I think, an art student. Her parents didn't live in Nottingham, though."

"Then how did you know them?"

"They came to me, asking for help," he said. "I gave them the name of a nursing home. It doesn't exist anymore," he said, quickly, seeming to cover his tracks. "*Wonderful* idea, adoption. Without it, the baby would suffer, you see. I think your father's people were Jewish," he added, whispering. He reached over and held my hand. I wanted to withdraw it but thinking he was about to confide something important, I leaned in. "Nothing to worry about, dear." He stroked my hand like a father of the church consoling one of his sheep. "You were a special case . . . came from two good families . . . no criminals, nothing nasty." He leaned back and released my hand with a sigh.

I thought to myself, *You could be from Mars for all you understand why I'm here.* "Nothing nasty" was not why I'd traipsed thousands of miles to sit in his gloomy office. I'd come for information, data. I was an adult, and *I'd* be the judge of what was nasty and what wasn't. He was treating me as if I were a child. I felt like shaking him. But instead, I girded myself Perry Mason-style and asked him where Eve went after she'd had me.

"Who's that, dear?"

"My mother," I said calmly.

"And how is your dear mother? It's been years since I've seen her! Is she still in England, did you say?" His evasiveness shocked me but I kept my head.

"My birth mother, Eve Wright. Where did she go?" I asked again directly, no holding back. He smiled as if I hadn't spoken at all. I said I thought he knew something he wasn't telling me. He waved his hand self-importantly, dismissing the matter.

"She married and went abroad. So long ago, don't remember. Come, you must be going. I must show you the gardens before you leave. We do have such lovely gardens in England, you must admit." He floated out of the study, a pontificating cloud of jangling vestments, leaving me alone, surrounded by his ancient books, his dusty church life, his narrow prejudices. My intuition told me that she didn't go abroad. She stayed in England. Was this intuition or was I simply angry? It was difficult to tell. What would Perry Mason do now?

That night, Gerrie and I ate fish and chips in front of the TV and watched *Coronation Street,* an English, working-class soap opera that had been running for years. Moo always hated it and made me turn it off. She didn't like its dreary theme song and the Midlands accents she'd left behind when she married Roger, my adoptive father. Though she had never returned to Nottingham while I was growing up, she often reminisced about it. Again and again, she told the story of how her parents took her every summer to Goose Fair, about the carnival rides, and the displays of cows, sheep, and ducks, and the long, wonderful summer nights that never ended. Besides a few childhood pleasures, though, Nottingham seemed to remind Moo of something she wanted to forget. She never told me what it was, but she had no intention of returning once a week via *Coronation Street.*

I told Gerrie about how I'd tried to talk to Canon Ingles' wife about my adoption before I'd left the church that afternoon. How she had refused to even acknowledge my presence. How Ingles himself ushered me out of the front door with a firm hand on my back.

"I always thought Ingles was a bit of a puffball," said Gerrie. "Your mother doted on him but then . . . " She broke off, not wanting to criticize Moo. I knew how easily my mother was flattered, especially by men, and Canon Ingles was a master of paternal comfort, which she had probably found flattering. As far as I was concerned, during his condescending reception he'd entirely missed the point.

"Yes," I said with pleasure, "a real puffball."

I had one more mission to carry out while in Nottingham: to look for my birth father, Philip. When I told Daddy I was beginning my search, he'd sent me a copy of my adoption papers and a note that said, "I hope everything goes well on Wednesday," referring to my appointment with the counselor, Mr. Day. Daddy was a proper British gentleman who kept his own counsel, but in his quiet way, I knew he'd given me his blessing to start searching. A native of Norfolk, not Nottingham, he had met Moo when he was social secretary of the Students Union at the University of Nottingham and Moo was secretary to the Vice-Chancellor. He didn't remember as much about the layout of the city as Moo would have done, including the name or location of my birth father's store, but Moo and I had been estranged for a few years. We'd had a stupid argument in Italy in which she sided with her Italian husband and I had responded rudely. With damaged pride on all sides, I had beaten a hasty retreat from the family farmhouse to a pensione and not a word had passed between us since.

To support my search, Daddy had tried to loosen the rusty wheels of his memory and given me directions to where he thought Philip's family business might have been. But I had neither the shop name nor Philip's last name—if indeed his first name was Philip—nor an address. All I knew was that I was looking for the trace of a small, Jewish-owned haberdashery that had been in existence in the City of Nottingham twenty years ago and might have long since closed. I wasn't too hopeful of success.

Following Daddy's directions precisely, I found myself at the bottom of a hill where two busy streets intersected. In the location where my father thought the shop might have been stood a traffic circle and a five-story car park. Nottingham had changed in twenty years. I sighed and pondered the hill. Since I was here, I might as well investigate, but I did it with a doubtful heart. I walked up and down the hill, asking window-washers and shop owners if anyone had heard of a Jewish haberdashery that was once at the bottom or the top of the hill, name unknown, but no one knew anything.

Positioned halfway up the hill was a small synagogue. I walked in and looked around. It was the first synagogue I'd ever been in, quiet and dark. It seemed to be empty. There was no one there to ask. Wearily, I realized that having no name and address was an insurmountable liability. I must find out his name somehow. I was exhausted. I had no idea searching would be such a struggle.

Riding the bus back to London, weighed down by what seemed like an unsuccessful visit, I wrote a letter in my notebook to the Ingles, summing up the frustration I felt.

August 14, 1978

Dear Canon and Mrs. Ingles:

You may think I'm a nuisance but that's because you sit on committees, viewing these things "objectively." You sat on my adoption board. You're responsible to me, whether you like it or not.

Had the proper records been kept and made available, my need to know might have been satisfied. Since the information that is rightfully mine has been destroyed or removed, my curiosity—more than that—my passion to know where I came from has been honed. What you dreaded, that I might actually trace my birth parents, is now my only avenue.

You know more than you admitted. I believe you deliberately tried to lead me astray. It is a spiteful way to behave and I am angry with both of you. Still, you have every right to your archaic notions.

Suffice to say that your well-meant evasions have not discouraged me. On the contrary, you talked to me and saw a determined person. I intend to investigate the circumstances of my birth so I can learn what you insist I should forget.

Sincerely,

Nicole J. Burton

I never mailed the letter.

Back in London, I returned to the Register Room at St. Catherine's House. People were searching, tracking down information on births, deaths, and marriages. I knew my way around now. I went straight to the big black marriage registers and pulled them off the shelf with a quiet fury, one by one, beginning with August 1956, the month following my birth. Each register covered three months. At *Jan Feb Mar 1957*, I waited impatiently until another patron finished his copying.

To kill time, I wandered back to the Births section and looked up my adopted sister, Christobel: *Oct Nov Dec 1960*. There she was: "Julie A. Hill, born in Hastings, [5h 286]." I copied down the citation to send her a postcard, though she had never been interested in searching. Why was I intrigued and driven, and she not at all? Why was my adopted sister, with her angelic English complexion and carefree giggles, so different from my dark introspection? We had been raised in the same family; was it a force of lineage that steered us to separate fates? I knew only the strength of the undercurrent that felt as if it were towing me out to sea.

Back in Marriages, the man had re-shelved the register I was looking for. I lifted it onto the worn oak reading table and ran my index finger down the chronological list of names. My heart was racing as if I knew she were nearby. I could almost hear her calling my name. I had to slow down my tracing to make sure I didn't miss her. I wanted to be scrupulously thorough. I didn't want to leave and feel later that I'd done a shoddy job.

Nothing.

I re-shelved *Jan Feb Mar 1957* and pulled down *Apr May June*. Nothing. Volume after volume, I traced the names down the avenue of one side, up the boulevard of the next. *Oct Nov Dec 1957*. My finger stopped as my eyes took in the entry: EVE WRIGHT married DEREK GOODMAN in Nthmbld. W. [1b 704]. Leaning against the reading table, I felt satisfied knowing I had been right and Canon Ingles had been wrong, at least in part. She had married but she didn't go abroad; she stayed in England.

Even before I looked in the births register, I was sure I'd find a half sibling born the next year. My mother's middle initial was missing but the name was unusual enough I wasn't concerned.

Now that I'd found Eve, I relaxed into the rest of the search. I went for coffee at the cafe next door and returned to check the entry again. It hadn't changed. I went back to Births and looked for her birth entry, remembering she was twenty-three when she had me, therefore born sometime in 1933. She was thirteen years younger than Moo. I found her: Apr May June 1933, "EVE L. WRIGHT, mother's maiden surname BARLOW, District of Yardlow [7b 822]." Moving along, I began looking for my siblings— my siblings. My family.

Considering that she might have been pregnant when she married, I searched the registers for Goodman births nine months from my birth, April 1957. Persistence paid off. After two hours of searching, I had assembled my whole family. Goodman children registered between 1957 and 1964, born to Mrs. Goodman nee' Wright:

MARTIN GOODMAN, District of Deptford, Jan Feb Mar 1958
KAREN A. GOODMAN, District of Fullham, Jan Feb Mar 1960
CRAIG B. GOODMAN, Nthmbld S., Oct Nov Dec 1962
NEIL J. GOODMAN, Nthmbld S., Apr May June 1964

I looked through four more years of registers, but four children (five counting me) seemed to be enough for Eve; there were no more. I was tired by the time I copied down the last citation. Hours had passed since I'd arrived, and I hadn't had anything to eat. Before I left, I ordered a copy of Eve's marriage certificate and Neil's birth certificate, which would give me the most recent address in the records. A grand day's work, I thought, as I boarded the train taking me back to my friend Fiona's flat.

The next day, I took a cut-rate coach called the Magic Bus from London to Paris to meet American friends. As I left England, I was spent but relieved. I hadn't found my birth parents, but I was on their path. Some people had been forbidding, true, but others had been encouraging. I could wait until my next visit to continue where I'd left off. Time would be my friend or so it seemed. In my notebook, I wrote:

"Forget the past? I wish I could. That beveled jewel, chipped, clouded, a relic. Forget the past, it's gone. I *can't* forget what I don't know. But I am beginning to feel involved, no longer a detached adventurer. The day belongs to me. My search is *real*."

I'd ordered the information I needed to continue. It might even be waiting for me on the hall table by the time I returned to the States.

Chapter 3

The documents were not waiting when I arrived home to Washington, D.C. and when they showed up in brown envelopes, they proved both disappointing and intriguing. My birth certificate contained nothing I didn't already know, except an address that meant little to me, 25 Bridge Street, Beeston, Notts. Eve's marriage certificate, however, was rich in new information. Under "Rank or Profession," it showed that her husband Derek was with the "River Police" and that she was a "Comptometer Operator," which I imagined had something to do with adding machines and accounting. This was deflating and didn't jibe with her being an art student, which was what Canon Ingles and Moo had both thought, but I'd secretly wondered if that story had been told to make me feel more special. After all, "Comptometer Operator" didn't conjure up the most exciting profession in the world, but it did fit with my sense of who Eve really was, a Midlands girl longing for family who'd experienced a bad start. The marriage certificate showed their parents' names and two addresses up north, his in Newcastle and hers nearby in Prudhoe on Tyne. The "River Police" must be the Tyne River Police, forty miles south of the Scottish border, I reasoned. I had been to Scotland only once, arriving in Edinburgh during Christmas break with a college friend. We both immediately caught the flu and spent most of our week beneath a comforter in a room so cold you could see your breath at midday.

I intended to return to England the next year to follow Eve and Derek's trail but life worked several unexpected turns, in art—I formed a community theater company—and in health—I was attacked by a stranger and didn't travel or work a regular job for a couple of challenging years. While recuperating, I visited the Library of Congress where they stored telephone directories from around the world. After describing my search to the research librarian, she gave me a stack pass and showed me where the directories were kept, a windowless storeroom between two floors crammed with rows of dusty bookshelves. Of course, the LC didn't have *all* the world's phone books, but I found several Newcastle listings in a 1977 Northumberland book: two D. Goodmans and one D. R. Goodman. In a brand new 1983 directory I found what I was looking for: D. Goodman, River Vw, The Eals, Shaggyford. The phone number was Haltwhistle 20032. It was the only D. Goodman in the book, but when I went home that day I didn't call Eve, nor did I the next day. I couldn't broach the distance in geography and between her heart and mine by phone. I put the number away until my next trip, which I hoped would happen as soon as I could organize my finances.

I worked for five years in the community theater, loving every minute but eventually my enthusiasm ebbed. Not that it wasn't still fun, but I was spending more and more time teaching and writing grants and less time producing and writing plays, my true love. I also had non-community play ideas I wanted to explore that weren't suitable for presentation within the company. I was bone tired of scraping together a living from insufficient grants and freelance writing. The arts grants we obtained only paid twenty-five cents on each dollar we needed. I imagined the Defense Department having to run its operations that way and shook my head. Most of my steady wages came from a house-cleaning business a friend and I had started because the theater was never able to do better than break even.

One day as I lugged home a portable vacuum cleaner, a neighbor stopped me in the portico of my downtown apartment building. We sat on the stone bench in front of the building, enjoying the long rays of afternoon sun. "You need a real job," said Steve. I crinkled my nose. Steve worked for the U.S. Department of Energy as a bureaucrat, and I had no intention of being lured into those gray halls. "I've applied for a research job and another running a training program for women," I said, hoping to cut him off before he started in on me again. Steve was always trying to "help" me.

"Come in on Monday morning," he said, "and take the typing test. That way if these other jobs don't pan out you'll have something to fall back on. You can type, can't you?" He sounded so condescending. "Of course I can," I said. I knew he meant well, but becoming a temporary clerk-typist was not what I had in mind after five exhilarating years running a theater, but to placate him, I agreed to take the test. Steve was already planning where he'd take me for a celebration lunch. "You'll like the office, Energy Emergencies. It's a great group of people, you'll fit right in. And hey, you'll get to work with me!"

I didn't get any of the more promising positions I'd applied for; the Department of Energy job was the only one offered. As much as I didn't want to become a government clerk, I knew I was finished with cleaning other people's houses, and I couldn't seem to translate my theater experience into a paying position anywhere. All my good shoes were down at the heel and every decent article of clothing needed cleaning, so I took the job. To my surprise, I found the work interesting and even remunerative. Without dashing to the brace of part-time jobs I'd cobbled together to support myself, I had more quiet time to write, enjoy myself, and save money for a visit to England. In fact, as I descended into what I'd feared would become a personal hell, my life flourished. After a year my position was made permanent and I was promoted and given a raise. I was writing my own plays and had become involved with a young man who was also a "hyphenate" like me; by day, Jim performed magazine production but at night he was a rock 'n' roller.

I hadn't seen Moo since our unhappy visit in Italy years ago, although we'd continued writing letters. Her Italian husband had died in a car crash, and she'd returned to England alone. I wanted to visit her and finally thought I could do so without harboring unrealistic expectations. Equally important, I was ready to find my birth parents, not simply search for them. It hadn't been only the distance, the lack of money, and the turmoil of injury that kept me from searching. I just hadn't been prepared. I had dreamed of finding perfect parents who'd say all the right things and make me feel perfect too. The intervening years had blessed me with a few lessons in maturity and I was as ready as I'd ever be to face the real thing.

Something else happened that was important to my search. When Moo moved back to England, she visited old friends in Nottingham, her first visit in decades. Out of the blue, she wrote to me, "By the way, your birth father's shop is still there. The name is Minson's. It's on Upper Parliament Street."

Gaping like a fish, I sat on the sofa reading and re-reading her letter. Why had she chosen this moment to tell me his name, something she'd known her whole life? Why? Perhaps she'd forgotten the name until she saw the shop again years later. Probably she felt protective of our relationship. If she'd fed my curiosity with facts, I might have wanted to find my birth parents sooner, and where would that have left her? Was she also sending me an olive branch, a signal that couldn't be mistaken for another half-hearted apology in our rounds of bad judgment? I understood that giving me Philip's name was an invitation I couldn't refuse. It was a gift, a family heirloom she'd waited years, consciously or not, to reveal.

In the spring of 1984 when I was 27, I visited Moo in Norwich. I discovered a quaint, blustery city in the southeast of England that clung fiercely to its crumbling medieval wall and narrow, winding streets. Three hours from London and an hour's drive from the North Sea, it faced east like a Saxon soldier and year round received the bitter blows of the Arctic wind.

"There's nothing between us and Siberia," Moo grumbled, pulling her camel coat tightly around her. It was May. Blossoms were on the apple and cherry trees and the spring flowers bloomed vividly despite the harsh weather. Moo had recently moved from another part of Norfolk into the City proper and we explored it together, seeing the sights and visiting the famous pubs and churches. "They say we've a pub for every day of the week and a church for every week of the year," she told me, and she wasn't far wrong. Off the beaten track for tourists, the stone city shone.

We decided to take an overnight trip to Nottingham. We were excited for this would be our first visit together, a couple of Nottingham girls going home. She knew I'd come to visit her and continue my search, and like the old days of long nature rambles and market prowls, she was game for the adventure.

Nottingham was a good three-hour drive from Norwich. We planned to stay the night somewhere and return the following day. By American standards, this was an ordinary distance to travel but it was deemed unusually long by some of Moo's friends. "Packed your trunk, have you?" asked Moo's friend Lily, only half in jest when we bumped into her at the market.

I was watching TV in Moo's sitting room when I casually mentioned the subject of finding Philip. "Do you think we could find the haberdashery?" I asked.

"I know Nottingham like the back of my hand," Moo said, hand on her hip and head thrown back. "I can tell you *exactly* where it is—Minson's, Upper Parliament Street, on the corner. I can see it in my mind like it was yesterday."

"Would you come with me?" I asked.

"Of course I will," she said.

"I mean, I don't know what will come of it. I'm not even sure he's the one. . . "

"I am," she said. "We went there when you were just a baby." This was part of the old story; I let her retell it. "After we got you, they told me he was the father."

"Who told you?" I asked. "His name's not on the adoption papers."

"I don't know, but I knew it was true," she said, brushing the details off like crumbs.

"Who told you? You must remember. . . "

"Well, I don't, and that's all there is to it." She lit a cigarette and inhaled.

"Go on," I said, letting the point drop.

"We went in, your father and I. We wanted to see if we could see him."

"Who?"

"Anyone. Your father, his father, your grandmother. So I could tell you about them."

"And?"

"He wasn't there, but your grandfather was. I saw him."

"You didn't say anything?"

"No," she said. "I bought a spool of thread." She looked at me with eyes twinkling with conspiracy.

"What did he look like?" I asked.

"An older man, Jewish."

"What else? What did the store look like? Was there anyone else there?"

"That's it. It was just a haberdashery but well known in Nottingham. My father used to be jealous of the Jewish merchants. He was a clothing salesman. Anyway, I'd seen him and that's what was important."

"Why?"

"Don't be silly. I wanted to be able to tell you so you would know where you came from." Upper Parliament Street, evidently.

"What about my mother?" I asked.

Moo inhaled deeply. "She was an art student, but I don't know anything about her. Now, clear the table for lunch. Would you like soup and a Marmite sandwich?" This was as far as she'd go, perhaps as far as she could go. It was a gift, even if some of the facts slipped down between the cushions. I was keenly aware she didn't have to tell me, and she didn't have to take me there. Though I felt she owed me this, many such debts are never settled.

We left early in the morning, waving goodbye to her friends at the county council flats. We stopped for a pub lunch in Long Sutton near the Wash, an inlet of the North Sea. The wind was fierce as we drew closer to the water. We struggled out of the car. The gale slammed the car doors and ripped the hats from our heads. We laughed but the wind tore the sound from our throats. In the quiet pub, we were the only customers.

"A might blowy, ay?" said the publican.

"There's nothing between us and Siberia," said Moo.

"But at least the sun's up and about," said the publican. He spoke with the broad dialect of the Midlands. What a tolerance the English have for poor weather, I thought, as we ate cheese sandwiches and pickled onions. Moo had a barley wine to "fortify" herself.

I drove west into the Midlands, and the weather became milder as if bestowing a benign blessing on our adventure. Nottingham again struck me with its sprawling size. The River Trent wound through the southern edge, spawning half a dozen solid bridges. Traffic hurtled through the industrial sectors and was tamed into one-way streams in and out of the city center. Make a wrong turn and you had to go all the way out of the city and start again.

As we found our way downtown, Moo pointed out places she remembered. "There's St. Peter's, where your father and I were married. Dear old St. Peter's. Canon Ingles married us. There's the bookstore where I worked. I must show you the bookstore. That's the road for Sherwood. We'll go up there this afternoon to see Rosemary for tea. There's Lower Parliament Street, you'd better park or we'll miss it."

We parked and walked back into the center of town where St. Peter's Church stood in the small square, surrounded by busy streets of shops and offices. Remembering my last encounter with Canon Ingles, I hoped Moo wouldn't suggest we drop in on him and she didn't. "Come on, it's up here," she said after we reached Lower Parliament Street. "I'm coming," I said, slowing down as the moment of reckoning approached.

"Look," she said, turning around to face me, arms folded in front of her, "we'll go in, you'll ask for Philip Minson and take it from there. If he's there, I'll run over to the pub and meet you later so you can have a private chat. You haven't lost your nerve, have you, darling?"

"No," I said, "but I'm nervous."

"*Coom on, duk,*" she said, slipping her arm through mine and talking in Nottingham dialect. "*Y've nuthing' to be afraid of. We've just coom t'buy soom thread.*" Upper Parliament Street was directly above Lower Parliament Street. We hiked up the steep hill. "There it is!" exclaimed Moo, "Just as it's always been." The shop was large and stood on the corner of the busy street at the top of the hill. Blue and white signs proclaiming "Minsons" ran along the top of the windows. "Fabrics, Linens, Curtains," read the sign in smaller letters. We crossed the street.

"Nothing ventured, nothing gained," said Moo.

"Fortune favors the brave," I added and we went in.

"Home of the Minet" announced a sign, promoting the company's brand of lace curtains. A woman was cutting fabric for a customer. "May I help you?" she asked.

"I'm looking for Philip Minson," I said.

"He's not here right now. He's up at the factory. May I help you with anything?"

He existed and he was close by. "No," I said. "I really need to speak with Mr. Minson."

"Perhaps you have a telephone number where we could reach him?" said Moo.

"I'd be happy to ring him myself for you if you'd like," said the woman, helpfully.

"No, I'd rather have the number if that's all right," I said.

"Certainly," she said. She wrote the number down on a piece of paper and handed it to me. I picked up a promotional flyer on the way out. It was blue and white with a design of a curtain on it. It read

MINSONS of NOTTINGHAM
for Quality Fabrics and Custom made Curtains
Browse through the
LARGEST RANGE OF
FABRICS IN THE MIDLANDS

and I thought, that's my people.

"Aren't you going to ring him?" asked Moo. We were standing on the sidewalk outside a real estate office, trying to work out our next move. I looked at the pictures of houses for sale.

"I think I'd like to walk around for a bit first," I said. The truth was I didn't know what to do next. The social workers had told me I should use a third-party intermediary to investigate the situation and find out if he wanted to meet me. Being close to contact, I felt both impelled and resistant. Reality would soon overtake my fantasies and I wasn't sure I wanted that. Yet, I wanted it more than anything. It reminded me of the choice on a TV game show from my childhood: The Money or The Box... The Money or The Box.

We went to the bookstore and up to Rosemary's for tea. Rosemary was my godmother, another old friend of Moo's from childhood days. She had lived a middle-class English life in a pretty suburban house in Sherwood, with a winding stone pathway from the sidewalk to the front door and a vivid flower garden in the back. She was a widow and her children were married with families of their own.

Happily, Auntie Gerrie joined us. I hadn't seen her since my first visit to Nottingham. Moo chattered amidst her old friends and drank one too many sherries, but we had a pleasant reunion. "Your mother says you're searching for your birth father," Rosemary said after Moo left the room. "I hope you won't turn your back on Roger," she added. "He's been a good father to you." Everyone had feelings on the subject. Why shouldn't they?

"I don't intend to," I told her. "That's not why I'm looking. I . . . it's hard to explain. I've always wanted to know. I've always wanted to see people who look like me."

"Then what?" she asked.

"Rosemary!" interrupted Gerrie. "She's just curious, and with all the pussyfooting around by that Canon and the rest, I don't blame her." Gerrie had always been impatient with British reserve.

"I suppose we'll correspond and visit from time to time. I'm too old to have parents. I mean, I have parents. I'm grown, so I guess I'd most like to be friends."

We drove back to Norwich that night, without my having made the phone call. I'd got Philip's home number from directory assistance but I wasn't ready to call. We stopped in Grantham for dinner and had a sumptuous meal in the old castle. Our table was by the window in what was once the bedroom of a four-teenth century prince. Moo felt more comfortable knowing she'd be returning to her flat that night, and I'd done enough adventuring for one day. We relaxed over dinner and shared a bottle of wine.

It had been eight years since our last visit together. Much had happened. I'd been in and out of college, started the theater, been attacked, and was recovering. Her second husband had died, she'd moved back to England, and been homeless a while before finding her Norwich flat. We'd fought our separate battles and had scars to prove it, but that night, we put the differences aside and delighted in having a special dinner together. We'd had a good day, filled with old friends and new adventures. For once in our lives, we were an English mother and daughter on vacation, chatting about our outing and pretending to fight over the check.

After we returned to Norwich, I kicked stones around for days, scuffing my shoes and feeling cranky. I couldn't call and I couldn't stop thinking about it. I tried finding an intermediary but Social Services said I had to put my request in writing. I didn't think to ask Rosemary or Gerrie, and I didn't really know anyone else. Moo confronted me.

"Look," she said, "you've got to call. You want to call."

"I know but... "

"Don't `I know but' me. This afternoon, we'll go round to Lily's and you can use her phone. I won't listen. You can make your call." I knew she was right.

Lily received us with her apron on. "I made some tea," she said as we walked into her garden flat. She was my mother's best friend in Norwich. They treated each other at the pub and watched TV together. Lily let Moo use her phone, and Moo did errands for Lily, who was frailer than she. After a cup of tea, Lily showed me into her sitting room and closed the door. I could barely hear the two friends chatting in the kitchen.

I'd composed an introduction that with minor alteration would work as well for Philip as for Eve. I tried to strike the right note of interest and mature detachment, but there was no way around the drama of the situation:

"Hello? My name is Nicki Burton. I live in the United States, and I'm only in England another few weeks visiting family. I was born in 1956 and adopted. My mother's maiden name is Eve Langston Wright and I have reason to believe that you may be my birth father."

This speech was the result of much mental sifting and editing, and it seemed to me I'd winnowed out the chaff. I didn't want to seem overly needy or pushy or weird, just friendly yet businesslike. I dialed, and a woman answered.

"Minsons, may I help you?"

"Philip Minson, please."

"May I tell him who's calling?"

"Nicki Burton. He doesn't know me, though."

"Just a moment." I hung on the line rigid, not breathing.

"Hello," said a pleasant male voice after a length of time. "This is Philip Minson." I took a deep breath and made my speech from the piece of paper in front of me. There was silence on the line. Finally he said, "What did you say her name was? And how old are you?" My heart sank into my knees. It had never occurred to me he wouldn't know who I was, that he wouldn't even know I existed. I repeated the information. "Eve Langston Wright. . . and I was born July 25th, 1956."

I could hear his mind flipping through the Rolodex of time, flipping back fifteen, twenty, twenty five years to his youth. I couldn't stand the tension.

"Look," I said, "I'm coming through Nottingham on my way to London next week. Perhaps I could stop in to see you." I didn't care that I'd suggested a geographical absurdity. I *had* to get off the phone.

"You've obviously gone to a lot of trouble in your search," he said, pleasant but noncommittal. "I'd be happy to meet with you if that's what you want." I took down the address, and we set a time the following week and rang off. I was ecstatic. I'd talked to him. He didn't know who I was, true. But I knew he was the one, even if he didn't know it yet.

Buoyed by my success with Philip, I decided to go ahead and call Eve. I had narrowed her whereabouts down to a town called Lemington outside Newcastle-upon-Tyne, way up north. I'd drive up and see her, assuming she was agreeable. I could see her after meeting Philip or perhaps before. My itinerary could follow the changing winds of the search. I rang the number and a woman answered. "Hello?"

"Is this Mrs. Goodman?" I asked, using her married name.

"Yes, it is. Who's this?" She spoke with a north country accent.

"And was your maiden name Eve Wright?"

"Yes, it was. What can I do for you?" she asked.

Still nervous but no longer an amateur, I proceeded. "My name is Nicki Burton. I live in the United States and will only be in England another two weeks visiting relatives. I was born on July 25th, 1956, and was adopted, and I have reason to believe that you may be my birth mother."

Without missing a beat, she responded, "Oh, that couldn't possibly be the case!"

Astonished, I stumbled and repeated, "I'm looking for Eve Langston Wright of Nottingham. . . ?"

"Oh," she said, breezily. "I'm Eve Wright of Prudhoe on Tyne. Sorry." And hung up.

I sat on Lily's sofa stunned. The blue brocade slipcovers swirled about me. In my heart, a stone dropped to the bottom of a rough, murky sea. All that thinking about Eve's family, her husband Derek with the Tyne River Police, their kids. I had their marriage certificate, for heaven's sake. I knew the names and birthdays of their children, my brothers and sisters.

I sighed. The icy water at the bottom of the sea cleared. I saw what I'd done. I had thought, what would a woman do who'd had a baby and put her up for adoption? She'd get married and have another baby. I'd looked in the registers for the marriage of Eve Wright following my birth, and when I found it listed in 1957, I stopped looking. I never dreamed that there would be two Eve Wrights; it was a fairly unusual name. Then I remembered the missing middle initial. I should have kept looking through the registers. Instead I'd ordered marriage and birth certificates and gone straight to the telephone books for a current address.

For six years, I'd been searching for the wrong Eve Wright.

Though the water was terribly deep, the light at the surface reached the stone at the bottom. I knew what I had to do. My mind returned to the Register Room at St. Catherine's House. I had to go back to the beginning. I knew I could do it, but the weight of the water pressed down on me, clear from the top to the bottom.

Chapter 4

It wasn't hard to find the factory in the Lace Market. On the edge of the city, I crossed over a bridge and wound through the narrow streets until I found Number 3, Broadway. It was an imposing gray stone edifice with brass plates and heavy wooden doors. I parked the Peugeot rental car into a space at the side of the building and prayed I wouldn't be ticketed.

It was do-or-die time. I pulled open the heavy door. At the end of a long hallway was a receptionist's window. I passed a workshop on my right where fabrics were laid out for cutting. "I'm here to see Philip Minson," I said to the receptionist. "I have an appointment at 11."

"Just a moment," she said and picked up the telephone. Out of the corner of my eye, I saw him approaching. He leaned into the reception window.

"That's all right, Susan," he said, "I'm here."

He gestured down a corridor, "Hello. Won't you come in?" I walked into his office. The clutter of business lay in piles and stacks. On the windowsill was a framed photo of a young girl about twelve dressed in riding clothes and another of a blond woman with two young children perched on the desktop. A calendar with a scantily-clad woman on the wall next to the desk surprised me. What kind of man hangs such a picture in his office? A ladies' man, I thought. That certainly fit the bill. I sat down in a maroon leather armchair and he began to walk behind the desk.

"No," he said, and returned and sat down in a chair beside me, "I'll sit over here next to you." He was a nice-looking man, slim and tanned, dressed in a well-cut gray suit, and seemed at ease with himself. His hair was dark brown and curly. He also had a salt and pepper moustache. He looked like someone I'd seen before. "I'm sorry I didn't know who you were on the phone. This only happened once in my life. Since you rang, I've been thinking, and I remember clearly now," he said. I nodded, waiting and watching. He cleared his throat. "How did you find me?"

"My adoptive mother, Jean . . . "

"The one in Norwich?"

"Yes. She was from Nottingham, and when she got me, somehow she knew about your father's haberdashery, and she went to the store."

"Did she ever meet him?"

"No. She saw him though. Growing up, I knew I was adopted. I knew my grandfather had a store in Nottingham. I even came and looked for it once myself."

"Here in Nottingham?"

"But I didn't know the name of the shop. I walked where I thought it might have been, but everything was car parks and traffic circles. I even asked at a synagogue."

"Which one?"

"I don't remember. There was no one there to help. I didn't know who I was looking for."

"So how *did* you find me?" He was eager to hear the story and sat forward in his chair like a child. As I talked, I observed him, detached as a camera, and filed the footage away until later. He was watching me, too, but we were both trying to hold a normal conversation. I felt as if I were hallucinating. All those years of staring at myself in the mirror, trying to see behind my own eyes; my God, I thought, I've done it—I've climbed through the looking glass into the world beyond.

While my mental camera rolled, we continued talking.

"About a year ago, Moo, that's my mother, wrote me a letter. She was back living in England again. My parents are divorced. She'd come to Nottingham to see old friends, and out of nowhere, she wrote and said the store was still here and the name was Minsons and it was on Upper Parliament Street. That was the first time I heard your name."

"Did you go there?" he asked.

"Before I rang you."

"I thought you were in Norwich."

"I was but I was here last week as well." We sat silently as he took in the intricate path of the search with its lacelike detail and handmade care. I saw the moment he realized I'd been shadowing him, I saw the idea cross his face. Yes, I've been following you, I thought, I had to, but I mean no harm. Could he sense this, I wondered. His brow relaxed. Yes, I imagined he could.

"So, then, you went to the store on Upper Parliament Street?"

"They gave me your number here. I wanted to get someone else to call, but it was too complicated, and. . . I didn't want to wait till my next visit. I'm only over here every few years. So I rang." As we talked, I compared our features. Eyes and nose were the same. Hair, a little curlier than mine. Hands, the same. Mouth, not mine. His complexion was darker than mine, but here was where I got my olive skin. Here were the eyes behind mine. A hundred scenes of solitary gazing flashed before me.

"What about Eve? Do you know where she is?" he asked.

I related the sad story of looking for the wrong Eve Wright. "I'm afraid I don't remember a lot about Eve," he said. "I don't know how much you know."

"They told me she was from Nottingham, an art student," I said.

"That's right," he said, "she was. And her parents owned a pub somewhere. God, I haven't thought of that old pub in. . . " He paused.

I completed the sentence for him. "Twenty eight years." As much as I already felt for this man, I was still irritated that he didn't remember me.

"Yes. It was somewhere outside Nottingham. I used to go and fetch her on Friday nights and we'd go to the movies." He stopped and searched for the right words. He was struggling; I wasn't going to help him on this. "It was not a great romance, your mother and me, but it was respectful," he said finally. He paused and looked at me, wanting to give me something. Was it an apology? Acknowledgement? Their relationship was what it was. I smiled and accepted it.

"She was very pretty and lively, your mother, always doing or saying something surprising. We broke it off for some reason, I don't know. I started going out with a friend of hers or she with a friend of mine, I don't remember. When she wrote to me, months later, to say she was pregnant, I was shocked. It was awkward. I was . . . engaged to marry someone else in three weeks. I told my father. He gave me some money and told me to go away for a week. I think he went to see her parents. Anyway, when I got back, it was never mentioned again. I'm sorry, I forgot all about you until you rang. I'm really sorry."

I heard him. I was listening. But the sense of being completely forgotten stung. It was an unexpected humiliation. To each of us, our lives are central. We're born, grow up, have joys and struggles, work, create art perhaps, marry, have families perhaps, and eventually die. How easily a single existence could be overlooked. How easy it had been for him to brush aside what my life would mean, like a speck of lint, as if I'd never happened.

I grieved for how things might have been had Philip claimed me and Eve. My heart burned. How could a man forget he'd fathered a child? Easily, apparently. Could Eve have forgotten me as well? Could she? I remembered each coin I'd ever dropped in deep water and each wish. I felt foolish. I had assumed my parents would remember me.

How long did I sit self-absorbed? He was still in the chair next to me, this man, my father of eight minutes. I couldn't describe the hurricane of feeling enveloping me, but I shook myself back to the present and saw a hopeful smile alight on his face. It was my turn to give him something. I had brought a message from Eve. "Did you know I was named after you?" I asked. "My given name is Pippa."

"No!" he gasped. "Why did you change it?"

I smiled ruefully, "I was renamed. Like a sailing vessel changing hands." I'd always loved my given name. Written in old-fashioned script on my adoption order, it was a stroke of originality given me by Eve, an affectionate diminutive pinned to my baby sweater, and a clue to my paternity. Pippa was also Pip, the young foundling character in *Great Expectations*. When Moo and I had been out together having fun, just the two of us, she used to link her arm through mine and recite the lines from Dickens' masterpiece, "What larks, Pip, old chap, what larks!" Bless her, she was the only soul in the world who ever called me Pip. In doing so, she acknowledged my real self.

As Philip and I crossed the street on our way to lunch, I asked him to tell me something about his family, and he began, "You know we're Jewish." How good it felt to be included. I did know, of course, but the "we" was very welcome after the emotional thunderstorm I'd been through in the past hour. We sat in a corner of the restaurant. I was exhausted. Whatever reserve of courage got me to Nottingham and in to meet Philip was totally spent. To stop from slipping under the table in a heap, I ordered a medicinal brandy with a nod to Moo and gazed blindly at the menu. Philip, thank goodness, was animated. He chatted about relatives' comings and goings and ordered lunch for both of us. As he talked, I pulled out a manila envelope from my purse and jotted down names, ages, and countries he mentioned. I knew I wouldn't remember everything, and that this might be my only chance to find out about our family.

"On my father's side," he said, "we're Russian. My grandmother, Rebecca, oh, you would have liked her. She was remarkable, tough, but she loved with the same toughness. She kept a market stall until 1980, till she died. She was 92. She came to England when she was 16. From Glasgow to Sheffield. She married and had her children young, and my grandfather. . . well, she raised those children herself, scrubbing floors, taking in laundry, whatever she had to do. She had come to this country alone from Moscow. I don't know where she was born.

"It's funny, with you living in America now. My grandfather went to New York City in the '20s, then Canada. He traveled like so many did, looking for his fortune. Came back to England broke. And two of my great aunts and a great uncle ended up in the States after World War II. Weisbord and Minsky were their names, and Stolnitz, a cousin of mine, I think he even lives near Washington. For a long time, the relatives living in California and the ones living in New York didn't know about each other. It wasn't till my great aunt went visiting a few years ago that they found out they were there.

"My mother's family came from Poland. Jews on both sides. Her parents came to England around 1901, 1902. I have an aunt who was the oldest of their children who was born in Poland, but my mother was born in England.

"My dad was a tailor. He started the business. He died in 1972 from cancer, but my mother's still alive. Longevity's on her side of the family. You can be sure, you'll live to be an old, old woman. She worked in the shop until a couple of years ago.

"Our name was originally `Minsky.' My grandfather changed it to `Minson,' I suppose because it sounds more English. They resented Jews in Nottingham in the textile business. I've got a cousin who changed her name back to `Minsky' though. Uncovering her roots. In fact, my eldest daughter even mentioned that to me once.

"Averill and I have two children, Louis and Rebecca, they're five and seven. It's my second marriage. The woman I married after I broke up with Eve, it was a disastrous marriage. We had one daughter and then we divorced. I was alone for a long time before I met Averill. She's twelve years younger than I am.

"The family was traditionally Jewish. My mother would have had a fit if I'd married Eve. But to tell the truth, I think I might have been much happier. You know, I was the oldest son, and so on, and the woman I married was technically Jewish, but it was a complete fiasco. . . ." He trailed off, alone in the memory of the failed relationship. I listened, took notes, and ate my sandwich, basking in the glow of reunion and accomplishment. "But come, I've been doing all the talking. You must tell me more about yourself, what you're like, where you've been."

I started to tell him about my life. Having just come from Moo's house in Norwich, I had some old photographs she'd given me. I spread them out on the table. He picked up the photo of me as a baby, sitting in Moo's lap, clutching her finger and staring intently into the distance. "Look at that Minson hairline!" he said. In the photo, my dark curly hair arched back to my temples as it still does. "That's what mine did before it started disappearing," he said. There were two pictures taken at my christening, one showing my brother Alan and Moo's father and the other showing Daddy. Philip took the photo of my father and studied it.

"He looks like a nice man, your dad," he said quietly.

"Yes, he is." My adoptive father was a generous man. He'd given directions to help me find the nameless haberdashery. He'd always supported my theater work, even if he thought I ought to be spending my time building a more conventional career. He was an accepting person long before the concept hit the popular press. There was another photo of me playing in the sand on a beach, and two of Moo's second husband.

"Your parents divorced?" he asked. I nodded.

I drew some papers out of the manila envelope and showed him the adoption order and new birth certificate and talked about growing up an "Air Force brat" with my father in the Royal Air Force. The waiter took our plates away and we had coffee. "Don't you need to get back to work?" I asked.

"No, I told my assistant you were coming. Even my wife dropped by today. She was curious, I think, hoping to bump into you. I'd like you to meet her and the children." His eyes dropped to the table in front of us. It was strewn with photos and papers. Lunch was over and the place was quiet. Suddenly, he pointed at the address on my birth certificate. "That's it! That's the pub! Beeston, Nottingham. That's it! Do you want to go and find her?" I didn't have to be asked twice.

Chapter 5

We hurried to my rental car and I rummaged in my bag for keys. "Runs in the family," he said, "I can never find mine either." As we set off, I thought, here I am, sitting inches from my birth father, a man who is also a total stranger. It was a strange but thrilling sensation.

"Go out here and make a left. It's all coming back to me," he said excitedly. We drove a long way into the Nottingham suburbs. "You know," he said, after a stretch of silence, "you were lucky to find me alive. I had a massive heart attack a few years ago. I was forty eight." I chewed on that fat piece of news for several miles. If I had arrived and found him gone, would I have had the gumption to talk to his wife? It would have been awkward introducing myself, "Hello, I'm the illegitimate daughter of your dead husband."

"Slow down and turn right. We're here." We had arrived in the sleepy town of Beeston. Not much to it—small rows of houses, a few shops, and on the corner, the pub. "I'm going to say we're old friends of Eve's. It's true, isn't it?" he said. "And we want to look her up."

I followed him in. It was a traditional British pub with a worn wooden floor and a circular wooden bar. Glass beer mugs hung from the top of the bar. There was a no-frills men's side and through a doorway, a carpeted lounge where the ladies and families congregated. It was past two o'clock. Both sides of the pub were almost empty and the proprietor was cleaning up. It was afternoon closing time.

"May I help you?" the publican asked. He looked to be in his mid-forties.

"I hope so," said Philip. "We're old friends of Eve Wright. Her family used to own this pub. Are they still the owners?"

"Oh, we've had the pub since '67. Bought it from the Wrights. They had it for years. Old Mrs. Wright still lives around here. I couldn't say anything for a daughter though."

"Can you tell me how I might find Mrs. Wright?" asked Philip gently. As I stood by his side, I was quite proud of him. He was as cool as could be.

"You might try Mrs. Brown over there in the houses on Frederick Road. Past the traffic light, second on the left. Number 16. Mrs. Wright owns her house, the one next door as well. She's a bit deaf, you know, but she's sure to have Mrs. Wright's address." We thanked him and walked outside.

"Off to see Mrs. Brown then," said Philip. He paused and looked at the pub for a moment, backtracking through time. "Hasn't changed much."

A row of ten small brick houses stood on Frederick Road. We knocked at number 16, but there was no answer. Philip walked to the end of the block and disappeared. I followed him into the back yards that stretched in a line of continuous green, broken only by flower beds and clotheslines. Two old ladies were folding sheets.

"I'm looking for Mrs. Brown," said Philip, approaching one of the ladies. They smiled and continued folding the sheet between them.

"Mrs. Brown?" shouted Philip into the face of the closest woman.

"Pardon?" she said.

"Are you Mrs. Brown?" he shouted.

"No, I'm Mrs. Turner. That's Mrs. Brown but you'll have to shout because she's deaf," said the woman. She tugged at her friend's sleeve and spoke right to her face.

"This gentleman wants to talk to you, Mabel."

"What? Who is he?" asked Mrs. Brown.

"Who are you?" asked Mrs. Turner.

Philip smiled and bent down toward the old lady. "I'm an old friend of Mrs. Wright's daughter, Eve. Do you remember Eve?"

"Who?" asked Mrs. Turner.

"Eve Wright. Mrs. Wright's daughter. Mrs. Wright, who owns your house. They used to have the pub," said Philip.

Mrs. Turner nodded her head, knowingly. "He's looking for Mrs. Wright," she shouted at her friend.

"Who?" asked Mrs. Brown. Philip turned and looked at me.

"Mrs. Wright, you know, Mrs. Wright," repeated Mrs. Turner.

"What about her?" asked Mrs. Brown, finally.

"What about her?" repeated Mrs. Turner to Philip.

"We want to get in touch with her," said Philip, relieved to move on in the conversation. "Do you have her telephone number or address? We're old friends of the family."

"Old friends of the family," said Mrs. Turner to Mrs. Brown. "They want Mrs. Wright's address."

"Oh, yes," said Mrs. Brown, "I have it written down inside." We both grinned, relieved. "But is he looking for the old Mrs. Wright or the young Mrs. Wright?" continued Mrs. Brown.

"The Mrs. Wright who owns your house," said Philip.

"He said..." began Mrs. Turner.

"Was he friends with the old Mrs. Wright or the young Mrs. Wright?"

"The young Mrs. Wright, I think," said Philip.

"What did he say?" asked Mrs. Brown.

"He said it was the young Mrs. Wright he's looking for," shouted Mrs. Turner.

"That's good, 'cause the old Mrs. Wright's dead, you know," said Mrs. Brown.

"Mabel, they want Mrs. Wright's address. Have you got it?" Mrs. Turner glanced at Philip with a radiant smile. "She's a dear, you know. Ninety-three but deaf as a post."

"It's very kind of you to help," said Philip.

Mrs. Brown reappeared, waving a piece of paper. "I have the address, but it won't do any good," she said. "She's not there."

"Where is she then?" asked Mrs. Turner.

"A nursing home, I suspect. She was in hospital, but I don't know where she's gone now. The young Mrs. Wright he's talking about?" asked Mrs. Brown.

"I see," said Philip. "Can you possibly tell me of anyone who might know where the young Mrs. Wright is now?"

Mrs. Turner screwed her face up, thinking. "You might try the farm at the end of the next road."

"Whose farm is it?" asked Philip.

"Reggie's farm. His wife is Mrs. Wright's great niece. The old Mrs. Wright, you know. Yes, I'd try Reggie's, I really would," said Mrs. Turner.

"Thank you very much for your help," said Philip.

"Thank you," he shouted at Mrs. Brown. We both nodded our heads at her, and she beamed and nodded back.

Around the corner and down a few streets, the farmyard was full of mud and pigs. An attentive sheepdog guarded the gate, barking loudly and prancing around the gate as we got out of the car.

"Hello," shouted Philip, "anybody home?"

A stout farmer in tall rubber boots strode out into the yard, calling the dog back with a few firm commands. At the gate, his face turned mild.

" 'Afternoon. What can I do for you?"

Philip gave his "old friends" story again.

The farmer pursed his lips. "Urr. . . Eve Wright. . . she don't live around here, you know. But come in, my wife might be able to get you an address or a phone number. Them's her people, not mine," he added.

We made our way into the farmhouse. The farmer sat us in the living room, which looked as if people seldom sat there, and went to find his wife. Philip raised his eyebrows and looked at me. I raised mine back.

The farmer returned. "She says Mrs. Wright's in a nursing home, and she doesn't have a number for Eve, but she's calling her cousin to see if she can drum one up," said the farmer, sitting down.

"Dairy farm?" asked Philip.

"Aye, and beef, and eggs."

"What does a side of beef go for these days?"

"Well, that depends on the size and the cuts, you see," said the farmer.

"I just got a deep freezer," said Philip.

"Oh, then it's an economical way to get your meat," replied the farmer. The farmer's wife appeared.

"Hello," she said. "You're friends of Eve Wright? You know, she hasn't lived around here for years, but our cousin had her address in London. No phone though, I'm afraid." She handed a piece of paper to Philip, who had stood up when she walked in the room.

"Thank you so much," he said. "You've been most helpful. Do you have a card in case I decide on some beef," he asked the farmer.

"Give us a call any time, half side, whole side, special cuts," said the farmer, escorting us back through the gate. We walked to the car. Philip glanced at the paper and handed it to me.

"That's a good address," he said, "one of the better London neighborhoods. She's done well for herself."

By the time we drove back to Nottingham, it was time for me to leave. "Do you mind if I take a picture?" I asked him.

"No, please do. In fact," he said shyly, "wait a minute while I go inside and get my camera." He returned with his camera and a tall, attractive woman who was his assistant. We stood together while she took a picture of us, first with my camera, then with his. Then she excused herself and went back inside. I took two more pictures of him alone in front of his old Lace Market factory.

As we hugged goodbye, he said, "There's no doubt in my mind you're my daughter." Perhaps initially there had been; perhaps he had not believed Eve when she wrote saying she was pregnant with his child. Perhaps that was why he never contacted her and why he was able to forget. But as we stood side by side, there was no mistaking our resemblance or the kinship we felt for each other. I liked him so much. He wasn't perfect, he was human. But he was a very nice human, my father.

I said the last of several goodbyes and drove away. In the rear view mirror, I could see him waving until I turned the corner. I couldn't believe my good fortune in finding him. I'd imagined many scenes taking place but none of them approached the magic of what had just happened. And for him to help me find Eve's address. What a gift.

I felt light-headed I was so happy, almost ill. Alone in the car with no one to talk to, my mind raced forward then cut back on itself, reliving the moments of the past few hours. As I pulled out into traffic at the rotary below the Lace Market, I heard grinding metal. I'd caught the fender of a car already in the lane. We both pulled over. Fortunately, the scrape was minor and the man whose car I'd hit was understanding. We both decided it wasn't worth worrying our insurance companies over.

Somewhat sobered, I drove on, trying to concentrate while inside I was on a rollercoaster squealing with delight. I was driving on the wrong side of the road through rush hour traffic in an unfamiliar city on my way to an unfamiliar suburb. I was ecstatic, delirious. Even if I bombed out completely with my mother, I thought, fifty percent of my search is completely successful. What more could a person ask for? My mind flipped ahead on the calendar: When would I see him again? Would he call me? When would I meet his wife? When *would* I see him again?

As I entered another suburb of Nottingham, I started thinking what I'd say to Daddy, whom I was driving to meet. Fate had led him to be in England and Nottingham at the exact moment I met Philip. I wanted to tell everyone everything, but I didn't want to hurt his feelings by seeming too enthusiastic. I pulled up to the house. Daddy was visiting Anne, an old friend of his and Moo's from university days. Much of what was making me happy about meeting Philip I imagined might hurt Daddy: That I'd found the elusive connection I'd searched for and dreamed about; that he looked like me and sleuthed like me; that here was my blood and bone father, my face in the mirror, acknowledging me to himself and the world, that very afternoon, that very hour!

My English breeding and the cautious creed of closed adoption screamed at me to be careful and guard my family's feelings at all costs. To show the height of my joy would be the ultimate disloyalty. *And they could still send you away.* Of course, I didn't believe that but the old fears flashed like a neon marquis: adoptee. As I slammed the car door, I shut the lid on my elation and walked up the path to the front door.

Of course, Anne and Daddy were waiting for me and talking about my reunion. I described in rather flat terms how our meeting went, the positive impression I had of Philip, our general plans to stay in touch, and changed the subject as delicately as I could. We drank tea, ate cookies, and discussed the summer weather ("quite nice for May") and our upcoming trip to Cornwall. Despite my resolve, on the inside, the riotous celebration continued, and at the center of the hullabaloo, a happy, wild-haired eight-year-old in her best party dress was jumping all over the furniture, accompanied by equally elated versions of herself, from infant to teenager to young adult. They played musical chairs, blew noise makers, and ate slice after slice of rich chocolate cake on this, their first real birthday.

By the time we left, I was ready to burst—or collapse. Both my father and I had rental cars. We had decided to drive to Cornwall separately, where we'd turn his in and keep mine. I was supposed to follow his red Ford, and we made plans to stop in Stratford-on-Avon for the night though we hadn't booked a hotel. With that, we were off, winding through suburban streets toward the M1, the motorway that would take us south.

Alone again, I chattered to myself, reliving and imagining conversations with Philip. It was almost like being in love. Actually, it was *exactly* like being in love, the same excitement at seeing myself reflected in another human being's face, the same thrill and energy and magic. Through the suburbs we wound, my father leading, and me following closely behind. He made several turns, a left, two rights, and another left. I followed, thinking he was taking a short cut or had an old house he wanted to show me. Sure enough, he soon pulled over and stopped the car.

I parked behind him, but when he got out of the car, I did a double take. It was not Daddy at all but a stranger. I felt sick; somewhere, I'd mistaken my father's car for someone else's and lost him. The man locked his car and went into his house. My judgment was in shambles for sure; two lapses in as many hours. The joy seeped out of me like the air from a balloon, but after a few minutes of misery, I realized there was nothing to do but pull out the map and choose the best route to Stratford. How I'd find Daddy when I got there, I didn't know.

Driving the long stretches of anonymous British motorway, at first I was angry about losing my father. Then I was amused. The theme for the day was "Looking for Fathers." Found one, lost another. The steady hum of the engine was soothing; I soon felt resourceful. Daddy and I would somehow locate each other, and the remembrance of meeting Philip returned, giving me a warm and satisfied feeling.

After driving an hour, I pulled off the motorway in search of a bathroom and went into a pub. When I came out, I walked up the row of diagonally-parked cars to stretch my legs and plan my next move. I would pull off when I saw the first Stratford exit, park in the most logical place, and wait. Daddy, the physicist, would probably reason the same. Walking back to the car, a red Ford caught my eye. Sitting in the driver seat, pondering the map, was Daddy. "Hello!" I said and hurried up to the car.

"My goodness, there you are! I saw you veer off after that other red car," he said grinning. "I tried following you and drove round and around but it was hopeless." I gave him a hug. We were both tickled to have found each other by chance. It was a silent affirmation of our special bond: in case of emergency, we knew how to find each other. In true British fashion, not much said but much felt.

We found a place to stay for the night just south of Stratford. Dining in the quiet restaurant, Daddy asked me some tentative questions about Philip. Did I think that in any way I resembled him? What sort of ages were his wife and children? Were they aware that I went to see him? Of course, he was curious too. I wished I could talk to him as a friend and not be so guarded. Instead, matching my tone to his reserved inquiries, I talked briefly and uncomfortably about my experience. It was less threatening to talk to him about looking for Eve, just as it was easier to talk to Moo about looking for Philip. I felt so damned responsible for not hurting their feelings. After all, they'd done their best for me as parents. Wasn't that enough? Why should I want more than that? I told myself that their parenting and my need to search weren't related, but I knew that wasn't entirely true. Our relationships were complex, with many threads both smooth and knotted. What was clear was that I had broken all the taboos I'd formerly accepted, and I couldn't help feeling ashamed and selfish for pushing ahead with my search.

We muddled through dinner. I had no intention of turning back but I packed my feelings away into a tight parcel for the duration of the trip. There'd be time later to shake them out and display them like elegant silk scarves for my friends. On a journey, it's sometimes necessary to keep one's treasures wrapped for safekeeping. But alone in my room, I allowed myself a peek. I unwrapped a corner and peered at what I had accomplished on this first-time-in-my-life momentous day. The time of searching in the mirror for the eyes of someone who looked like me was over. I'd found them. I was related to someone who walked this same planet, someone kind. I was no longer alone in the world. I curled up in my single bed and cried.

Chapter 6

The next morning, I felt surprisingly clear-headed. Daddy and I enjoyed a leisurely breakfast and wandered the commons and bric-a-brac shops of Moreton-upon-Marsh, the little town we'd stayed in. The drive to Cornwall was pleasant and we stopped for a pub lunch on the way. Having traveled together often, Daddy and I fell into a comfortable rhythm, the excesses of the day before melting into memory.

We arrived in the Cornish town of Loue at suppertime. The town was divided by a bridge into East Loue and West Loue. We angled our way through the winding streets and over the bridge and found our hotel on the other side of the first bluff of West Loue. It was a noble, white-washed building that faced out to sea. The sun hung low on the horizon when we arrived and sailing boats tacked outside the harbor in the open sea. My father used to sail as a young man and we stood and gazed at the sailboats for a long time.

The next morning, when the tide was high, fishing boats motored out of the harbor in search of a catch. Sailing boats shot through the narrow mouth into open waters where they leaned full-sailed into the wind and raced each other along the coast until evening. As the tide receded around noon, the boats remaining in the harbor became grounded in the mud and listed ungracefully to one side while well-fed gulls picked around them for worms.

It was time for my next move. With Eve's name and address in hand, I tried calling but her telephone number was unlisted. This didn't surprise me, and I moved to Plan B. I sat in the lounge of our lodging and drafted a letter to her, which I passed to Daddy for his opinion:

May 20, 1984

Dear Eve,

I tried to call you, but your number is unlisted, so I am contacting you by letter. I recently met my birth father, Philip Minson, in Nottingham, and he helped me obtain your current address. I live in the United States and I am in England visiting my mother and friends and traveling around for another ten days.

I shall be staying in Cornwall at (telephone number) until the 25th, then I may be reached at my Aunt's house in Brighton at (telephone number) until the 27th, then I shall be back in London at a friend's house (telephone number) until I leave on May 31st.

If this letter should find you on holiday, my address in the U.S. is 1725 17th Street, #413, N.W., Washington, D.C.,

20009, U.S.A. I am happy and comfortable in my life and have no wish to disrupt yours, but if you'd like to meet me, I'd like to meet you.

Sincerely,

Nicki Burton
(Pippa)

Daddy read the letter and agreed it covered the essentials and left the door open for reply. Since I'd felt I had to detach regarding Philip, it was good to have my father involved in the search for Eve, and he seemed to appreciate playing a role. We wrote some postcards and drove into the center of Loue to mail them.

For the rest of my stay in England, thoughts of the letter I'd mailed percolated in my brain. Is she reading it? Will she answer me? Is she calling me at the hotel while we're out in the Cornish wilds looking for Camelot? Does she hate me? Will she like me? Is she there? My Eve antennae extended to their maximum length, and I swept the villages and countryside for signals all week long.

Thinking back, how honest had I been in my letter? Was it true that I was "happy and comfortable in my life?" Truthfully I'd ached to have a relationship with Eve from the beginning; she would be the stable, steady mother I never had. My nonchalance was a front, even to myself, especially to myself. I had not grown up feeling particularly lovable and half-believed that you had to trick people into loving you. If that were the case, my best hope of ensnaring Eve would be to feign indifference while charming her into caring for me as much as I already cared for her. It was a ploy I'd tried before with some success. The question was would it work with her? After all, what did I know about her? She'd been an art student, her parents owned the pub in Beeston, and she'd named me after my father. I thought about Philip. I wanted to call him, ask his advice. He'd asked me to call before I left England and I agreed, but as I closed in on my oldest acquaintance—a woman I'd never met but known forever—I decided to wait until after whatever was going to happen next.

Daddy and I spent five days in Cornwall then drove to Brighton to see his sister and family. After we arrived, we met my uncle and aunt at our hotel. Already, they had the news and wanted to know how my search was going. I filled them in on the story using a broad stroke and continued to wait on tenterhooks. I heard nothing. I spent several days being blown along Brighton's Victorian seaside promenade and returned with my father to London.

We stayed at my old friend Fiona's house in Teddington outside London. I had known Fiona since I went to boarding school in England. Miraculously we'd remained friends after my family emigrated to the States. She'd visited me in Italy when I lived there, and I'd stayed with her while I did research on my previous visit. We'd lost track of each other a few times, but I always called her when I came to England. A self-proclaimed non-letter writer, Fiona had valiantly corresponded when we were separated by oceans and cultures. We didn't even have much in common, but we still found ourselves good friends. After she'd married Trevor, a British Airways pilot, they'd bought a house, settled down and had a son, Noah.

Wherever I went, the phone sat silent. I'd never heard phones not ring so much. I had planned to stay on at Fiona's for a few days after my father returned home. In the rush of getting him and Trevor off to the airport the day after we arrived, I hadn't had time to fill Fiona in on the latest chapter in the story. We kept passing in the hallway and promising each other a quiet cup of tea, but between send-off logistics and children needing attention, it didn't happen. I was in my room writing a letter when the telephone finally rang. Fiona knocked on the door. "Nicki," she said, "it's for you."

"For me?" I asked, momentarily baffled at who could be calling me. Such is the power of denial.

"I think it's *her*," said Fiona. "Here, take it in our room." She ushered me into her bedroom. "I'll hang up downstairs." She hugged me and tiptoed out of the room. I picked up the receiver. "Hello?"

"Hello," said a clipped voice at the other end of the line.

"This is Nicki."

"It's Eve."

"Hello," I said. "You must have got my letter."

"Yes, I did. The first thing I want to tell you is that I don't want to get involved in your life . . . " I felt as if a boulder had dropped on my chest, knocking the air out of me. Pain radiated from my core.

". . . but I am curious," she continued. The boulder rolled and stopped. "So I should like to meet you somewhere if we can arrange it."

"I'd like that," I said, breathlessly.

"I have to be very careful. My husband doesn't know about you."

"I see. Perhaps we could meet up in London somewhere, someplace quiet."

"When are you leaving?" she asked.

"The day after tomorrow. So it would have to be tomorrow."

"That would be fine," she said. "Where shall we meet?"

I realized my London haunts amounted to a few rituals of shopping and theater. "How about the coffee shop at Miss Selfridge?" I asked. I hadn't thought through what I would actually do if she called me.

"Fine," she said, sounding relieved it would be so simple. "How shall I know you?" she asked. I couldn't remember a single distinguishing characteristic about myself and mumbled incoherently. "I mean, what will you be wearing?" she asked again.

"A beige linen jacket. And I have reddish-brown hair. How will I know you?" I asked.

"I shall be wearing a black jean jacket. I have blondish hair. I'm not very tall. Are you tall?"

"No, not very. About average, I guess."

"And you live in America?"

"Yes, my family emigrated there. I'm just here in England visiting . . . relatives."

"What time shall we meet?" she asked.

"How about afternoon, about two?"

"All right. I shall only be able to stay an hour or so. I have to go and pick my husband up from the airport. He's been on a trip," she explained. "I have to go now," she said, hurriedly. "Two o'clock tomorrow at the Miss Selfridge coffee shop."

"Right. I'll see you then." She hung up quickly.

She rang me. She wants to meet me. She doesn't want to be involved in my life, whatever that means, but she wants to meet me. I focused on the "wants to meet me" and threw away the disclaimer, much as I'd dismissed the middle initial when I examined the record books. I would win her over regardless of how she felt. As was my stubborn style, I didn't entertain any alternative.

Downstairs, Fiona had the tea waiting. "Was it her?" she asked, pouring me a cup.

"Yes. We're going to meet tomorrow in town."

"I knew it had to be her," Fiona exclaimed. "She sounded so . . . she sounds very proper."

"I think she's quite reserved. But she can't be that reserved if she wants to meet me," I said.

"You haven't told me what happened with Philip. And how did you find her?" We were deep into the search for Philip when the phone rang again. "Just a minute," said Fiona, covering the receiver. "It's her again," she whispered. Sure enough, it was Eve, apologizing for getting off the phone fast.

"I'd waited till my daughter left the house to call you, but she'd forgotten something and came back. I almost died. I just wanted to make sure we had our arrangements set for tomorrow," she said. This time, she sounded more vulnerable. We confirmed our arrangements and chatted for a few minutes. She told me she had three daughters, two in high school, and one in college. "I never told anyone about you," she confided. "Just one friend. So you see, it's difficult for me, hearing from you like this. But since you've gone to the trouble, I think we should meet."

Chapter 7

The next day I dressed in a turquoise skirt printed with colorful bouncing shapes. I wore my green sweatshirt, the one that brought out the color of my green eyes and made me feel lithe, and the identifying beige jacket. Fiona fussed over me and insisted on driving me to Teddington station. On the way into London, I gazed out of the windows at the grim, semi-detached houses on either side of the train line. There but for the grace of God.

I didn't think I was nervous; I suppose I was numb. I did realize life would never be the same but I was ready. I'd felt more anxious meeting Philip. I've done that already, I told myself. I don't need to feel that way with Eve.

The smell of the train grime, the rough-cushioned seats, the whine and rhythm of the wheels pulled me into the giant city; I had been there before, looking for her in the record books of St. Catherine's House, looking for myself in shop windows and museums, looking for my childhood, searching for the sights and smells of a Covent Garden, Piccadilly, and Palladium that didn't exist anymore. Except that they did, in the taste of the tea cakes, the smell of the tea, and the smooth feel of wooden benches in the waiting rooms of old British Rail stations.

Time waited for no man or woman on this day. The train pulled in, the doors flew open. Passengers surged out onto the platform, through the gate, and splintered into Victoria Station. Foreign students dozed in sleeping bags on the filthy station floor. Humanity of all classes and races hurried between the snack bar, the newsstand, and the taxi rank. Families with piles of suitcases stood waiting for Father, looking stranded. The loudspeaker reeled off the place names of my childhood, "Staines, Weybridge, Byfleet, Woking, Farnborough, Aldershot, Haslemere, Petworth. . ." We had lived in so many places in England that almost everywhere in the Home Counties—north to East Anglia and south to the sea—was home. "St. Albans, Luton, St. Neots, Huntingdon, Ely, Downham Market, King's Lynn, Norwich."

I tore myself away from the litany of places and caught the Victoria line Underground to Oxford Circus. I had been early but lost time dawdling in the station. The tube train was also crowded. Although it was not yet the height of the season, there were already plenty of tourists seeing the sights. I liked reading the advertisements in the Underground; they say so much about the country. Lots of ads for borrowing money, for gin, beer, American movies, Scotch whisky, and the omnipresent public service ads for milk. Ever since the milk supply had been contaminated by the Windscale nuclear accident in the 1950s, Her Majesty's Government had wheedled and begged the population to resume milk drinking. "A Pint Per Person Per Day," the ads exhorted. In English boarding school, we were not allowed to drink milk except to put in our tea. I'd assumed the prohibition was due to the expense but perhaps unconsciously people thought it was unsafe. At any rate, it took years of living in America to develop a taste for it. Movies. Plays. Gallery exhibitions. Magazines. Headache tablets. Bras. Cigarettes. The consumable culture of the capital was displayed in poster-sized advertisements in wooden boxes up and down the ancient escalators that hauled me to the surface of the city.

Selfridges, one of London's top-rate department stores, was a block away from the station entrance. I made my way through the Scarf department, through the Records and Stationery sections under renovation, and into Miss Selfridge, the boutique at the back of the store. The coffee shop was situated on a mezzanine overlooking the wide expanse of clothing. It was a pleasant place to rest after a hard shop, to sit and people-watch the mostly young women. Yet there were older women there too, meeting friends for a regular date, resting their sore feet in a familiar place.

I took a deep breath and passed through Accessories. At the foot of the winding, carpeted staircase, I looked up but didn't see anyone looking for me. At the top of the stairs, I looked around again. My heart was racing. It couldn't be that she wouldn't come. Perhaps she'd got nervous and cancelled at the last minute, and I'd already left the house when she rang. Maybe her plans changed and she had to pick her husband up earlier. And then I saw her, sitting at a table for two.

At first she didn't see me and I had a moment to observe her. She was pretending not to look around, remaining cool amidst the bustle of afternoon tea. She had wild, gray blond hair and wore a snappy black jean jacket and black jeans. She looked younger than I had expected, younger than Moo, still youthful and defiant in spirit I could tell from halfway across the room. She saw me and I smiled and walked over to the table.

"Eve?" I asked.

"Yes," she replied. I sat down. We chatted about nothing for a moment, getting there, the temperature, traffic. Finally, she said, "You look exactly like him."

"Yes, I do," I said, and what a joy it was to know with my own eyes that it was true.

"You don't look a bit like me," she said, looking me over. I couldn't tell yet if what she said was accurate. She wasn't pretty exactly but her face was striking, a generous nose, powerful cheekbones, gray eyes, and that unruly mass of blond hair. Her body was petite and shapely. I made mental note of these physical characteristics; perhaps this would be how I would look in middle age.

She wanted to know how I had found Philip, and I told her. She acted uninterested in him yet I sensed obvious feeling. Was it resentment, heartbreak, or plain old pain? She asked me what he said about the circumstances of my birth and smiled when I got to the part about how he'd reacted when she wrote to tell him she was pregnant. "It wasn't quite like that," she said and folded her hands without elaborating. I wanted to know. I sat across from her and watched. Please tell me, I thought. "The best way I can explain it," she said finally, "is to say it was the Fifties, puritanical, and I never felt like I fit in. There was a very good book by David Lodge called *How Far Can You Go?* I remember reading it a while ago and thinking, yes, that's just how it was. I was not a promiscuous girl, but I always had boyfriends. I was romantic, always falling in love, sensual. Couldn't finish things. I was much happier in the Sixties and from then on, I can tell you.

"Philip came from a conservative Jewish family, you know. His mother would have died rather than have him marry me." Her voice betrayed a trace of bitterness. "His family paid the bills, but I never heard from him, *ever*. When you were born, I remember looking at you. You didn't look a bit like me. I remember thinking, there lies a perfect stranger."

Though I kept my face immobile, she might as well have taken a paring knife and stabbed me in the heart. She dragged on her cigarette, looked at me then looked away. I gazed across the table and the miles of years between us. This was clearly how she had really felt but it hurt so much to hear her say it. What an odd woman, I thought. Still, I wanted her to feel at ease and give us a chance to get to know each other, to prove I wasn't a stranger but her daughter.

"Shall we get coffee?" I asked. We went through the self-service line, each pouring a cup of coffee. Food was unthinkable; we were both far too nervous to eat. We returned to the table, and she lit another cigarette, offering me the pack. "No, thanks," I said. "I quit last year. I was a hopeless fiend."

She smiled. "Good discipline then. I've never had much discipline. You're almost twenty-eight now?" she asked, as if she didn't know. I nodded. "And will you be home for your birthday this year?"

"Yes. I'm going to Spain and Germany, but I'll be back in the States by the end of June."

"I always think of you on your birthday, you know. July 25th," she said. I knew it all along.

"I think of you, too," I said. "I always knew no matter what you are doing all the other days of the year, on my birthday, you must be thinking of me."

She stared at me, thinking a private thought. "I only told one friend, a very dear friend who never breathed a word to a soul," she said. "But I have another friend whose daughter's birthday is the same as yours. I always gave her presents. Once she asked me, `Eve, how is it you always remember my birthday?'" I couldn't help but resent the thought of her giving my presents to another child. Yet I listened brightly to all she had to say, taking it in.

"Last year," she continued, "I was in Italy. I made a pilgrimage to the frescoes of Fra Angelico on your birthday." I knew the frescoes of Fra Angelico. I told her that my father had been stationed in Northern Italy and that I'd lived there as a teenager, that I'd taken a high school field trip to the frescoes she spoke of. She told me about her husband who owned a large textile company and traveled often in the United States on business. She had been to New York, to Washington, D.C., and North Carolina, even to Nags Head on the Outer Banks, one of my favorite beaches. We discovered we had probably been there once at the same time. It was uncanny how close our paths had come to crossing.

She asked me about myself, what I liked to do, where I worked. I told her I was a playwright with a small theater company. She asked me if I acted. "Sometimes," I said, "when drafted. I enjoy acting but it takes time away from writing, which I'd rather do."

"You could do well in the movies with looks like yours," she said, unexpectedly. "You'd stand right out even from the back row."

She'd complimented me. I felt shy and warmer towards her. I told her I was considering going back to school to finish my degree in literature.

"I *love* American literature," she said. "Not so much the colonial writers, but, oh, Emerson, Whitman, James, Wharton. I couldn't live without them! I have another daughter who writes," she continued. "And one who paints. The other one, I don't know yet. I think she likes business like her father."

"You were an art student, weren't you?" I asked her. "Somehow, my mother knew that because that's what she told me, but I thought it was made up, just a nice thing to say."

"I went to London Art College. I didn't finish my program but I've painted ever since. I don't know how good I am, probably not very," she said, trailing off. She lacked self-confidence, I observed to myself. I knew first hand how destructive it was to denigrate one's own artistic work. I made note to be on the lookout against this trait; perhaps it was genetic. I wanted to know more about her and the shape of her life. But I didn't want to scare her away with questions.

"Did you ever work, you know, a job?" I asked, gingerly.

"No," she said, "not really. I had you and. . . well, it wasn't a very happy patch in my life. I had a fiancé and we were on the verge of getting married, and he left me for someone else. I was pregnant again, so it was quite a shock. But I said to myself, "Eve, you can't go around leaving babies all over the place," so I kept her. That was my daughter Angela.

"When I met my husband Thomas, he fell in love with both of us and after we got married, he adopted her," she said. "Then we had two more daughters, Marianne and Jules—Juliet. Angela's the one who writes; Jules is the painter."

For a moment, I was transfixed by the idea of my sisters, all artists together, madly writing and painting, and there in our midst, swirling oils on a dark canvas, our mad matriarch. I smiled as she kept on talking. This was what I had come for, the connections, ciphers for the blood and passions coursing through me.

"I never told anyone," she said, "except my friend. Things were different. And then I was married, with the girls. What was I supposed to do? Sit down at dinner one night and say, 'Thomas, girls—I have something very important to tell you?'" Yes, I thought, that's what you should have done. What you still should do.

But instead I said, "I understand." Did I? I was saying what would soothe her, playing the caretaker. "I don't expect any-thing from you. I have my family. I have a boyfriend and a life of my own in America. I don't expect you to disrupt yours for me now." Lies, lies, lies. She waved off my words but looked re-lieved.

"Perhaps I shall write to you occasionally," she said with a regal air. "I could send you the name and address of my friend and you could send your letters to her house." There, my re-straint had paid off already.

"I would like that. By the way," I asked, "do you remember what time I was born?"

"God," she said, "why do you want to know *that*?"

"I want to have my horoscope done, but I need the time."

"You don't believe in that nonsense, do you?" she asked.

"How appalling. It was the morning, around eleven, I think. I don't remember exactly when."

"How old were you?"

"I was about... twenty three," she said.

"So now you are...?" I said, trying to compute it in my head.

"Age has never been important to me," she said with forced casualness. "I just had my fifty-first birthday on Monday." I quickly jotted down her birthday on the back of my manila envelope. I asked her if I could take her picture. She shook her head. "I look terrible in photographs, absolutely dreadful."

How disappointing. I would have loved a photograph of her. I liked the way she looked but evidently she didn't. She must have seen the rejection cross my face because she spoke again softly. "One of my daughters has taken a few pictures that aren't quite as hideous as usual," she said. "Perhaps I'll send you one of those." She looked at her watch. "I must be going. Will you walk out with me?"

We rose and walked down the stairs into the mass of clothes and shoes. She touched my shoulder. "You look as if you had a nice middle-classish upbringing," she said with her hand on the shoulder of my jacket. It was not an expensive jacket but well cut.

"Yes," I said, wanting to reassure her again. I understood she was relieved that I didn't grow up cold, hungry, and poor, every birth mother's nightmare. She was relieved, too, as we walked through the store, that I didn't want anything from her. At least I wasn't going to blackmail her immediately for cold cash or create some humiliating scene involving her family and station in life. Of course, I did want something from her; otherwise I wouldn't have come.

"I should think something in brown wool would look very nice on you and keep you warm in those fierce American winters." I was warmed by her desire to clothe me. Moo had been long gone by the time I was out of school uniforms and old enough to appreciate clothes shopping. We walked to the Underground station and said a brief goodbye. She gave me a hug and said she'd write. A second before she turned away, she said quietly, "I'll never leave you again, you know that, don't you?" I looked into her deep gray eyes and nodded, and then she was gone.

Afterwards I walked and walked. Down Oxford Street, looking in shoe shop windows. Up to Marble Arch, around the Serpentine Lake, over to Hyde Park Corner. I looked for a Lyons Corner House for a meal but they were all gone, victims of McDonald's, Pizza Hut, and changing times. I walked back along Park Lane, down Oxford Street and into the Golden Egg for an omelet. Watching the people pass by outside, I felt cold. I walked back to Selfridges, through the store, upstairs to the coffee shop, and sat at our table again. I got a cup of tea and as I drank it, I wrote some postcards. This was our reunion place; I had to be here. I thought about the brown wool jacket. I thought about her at the airport. I thought about my sisters and their jackets and her big house in Hampstead.

Downstairs, I eyed the shoes listlessly. Not today, but if not today, when? I was leaving the next day, so I forced myself through the ritual of shoe selection and bought a pair of red and black sandals to mark the occasion. I was exhausted.

I caught the Underground back to Victoria and segued nicely onto a suburban train to Teddington. The trip went much faster than in the morning. People minded their own business, reading newspapers and eating British Rail sandwiches. The countryside sped by, the lines of drying clothes, the garden plots and sheds, London's back yard. As it flew by, I was consumed with thoughts of Eve and her family.

By the time I hopped off the train at Teddington, with its tidy Edwardian homes and block of shops, I felt as if I had successfully passed another examination, untold hours, pouring over pencil and paper in a windowless room. The wind blew cold and fresh as I walked across the railway bridge. I had found my parents. I had finished my exam. I had passed. I turned onto Langham Road. Fiona's red car was in the driveway. The wind blew a bed of yellow, pink, and purple snapdragons in the front yard. My key slipped into the lock, announcing my arrival home. Fiona called from the kitchen.

"Hello, come in." She popped her head out into the hallway, wiping her hands on a dishtowel. "We're just sitting down to tea, aren't we, Noah? How did it go?" All of a sudden, I could barely take another step. "It went well," I said and shut the front door. In the kitchen, tea was on the table, and Noah was watching *Blue Peter* on television. I sat down and started sobbing. I told Fiona about my day, ate baked beans on toast, and drank some tea. By the time the evening news came on and she'd made a second pot of tea, I was beginning to feel restored.

Chapter 8

Ijourneyed to Paris to stay with a friend before traveling south on a romantic whim to Barcelona. I didn't know anyone in Spain, but I'd fallen in love with Barcelona after reading George Orwell's *Homage to Catalonia* about the Spanish Civil War and listening to Dylan's "Boots of Spanish Leather." I was a romantic like my mother. Before I left Paris, I called Philip.

"Are you having a good time?" he asked me. "I do hope so." I told him about meeting Eve and he was pleased it went well. "I was rather flabbergasted when you rang me the first time," he said, reflecting on our meeting. "But now that we've met and I've seen you in person, I hope you'll stay in touch. I'd like you to meet Averill and the children. I'll send you a photo of them, shall I? I was so very glad you searched me out, so very, very glad."

For the rest of my trip, I thought continually about Philip and Eve. I wondered if there would be mail waiting when I got back to the States. By the time I returned, I was bubbling over with expectation. Of course, everyone wanted to know what happened and what would happen next.

No letters or packages awaited me, which was disappointing, but the rest of the summer my mind was well-occupied with a new project, working with teenagers in my theater company. I never stopped holding my breath when I turned the key in the mailbox and I waited and wondered. Should I write? Should I wait to hear from them? I asked myself these questions endlessly. Finally I wrote to Philip and I waited to hear from Eve.

On my birthday, I reached into my mailbox, pulled out the contents, and a blue airmail letter fell to my feet. The back of the envelope was embossed, "M". The notepaper was printed with the name of his house, the village, and county, very English and rural:

Dear Nicki,

I was so pleased to receive your letter and to know that you enjoyed your trip and arrived home safely. Actually I would have replied sooner, but unfortunately I mislaid your letter to which I would have liked to refer. I still haven't found it, so must try and remember everything you wrote. I expect it will turn up soon.

He went on to give news of the weather, the water shortage, his vacation plans. Then, he wrote,

Your photographs arrived back from the developer yesterday. They are quite good, and Averill, my wife, thought you bore a strong resemblance to me. I regret that we did not have more time to get to know each other, and dearly hope that you may consider another trip to the U.K. and in

particular, to Nottingham, and perhaps consider staying with us. I would very much like this, and Averill also. I wish you had made yourself known to me years ago, and although I never thought about you at all before, I certainly am making up for it now.

Unfortunately, life rolls on, and we cannot predict what the future holds, so it would be so nice to make up for 'lost time,' if that is what you desire. My life is so tied up with work and family commitments, I would find it very difficult to visit you. My health at the present is good, but I can't vouch for tomorrow. Be happy and well, and please stay in touch.

Very much love,
Philip X

He included a photograph of my half-brother and half-sister, Louis and Rebecca. Ages seven and five, he was fair and she looked dark and determined. They were riding bumper cars at the carnival. Everything Philip had written, he'd said before, but being able to read it was a special joy. Committed in writing, I believed it more. His references to health reminded me of his heart attack a few years before. I realized he felt God's breath on his neck. I was concerned and determined to visit him again soon. Although he seemed unaware of my birthday, his letter was the best present I could imagine, or almost the best.

Hearing from Philip softened the blow of not hearing from Eve, who I knew remembered my birth date. I heard her ambivalent statement in my head: *"I don't want to get involved in your life but I am curious."* I hoped she was taking her time deciding how to approach our relationship. Sure enough, a week later a peach-colored envelope arrived, with Italian stamps, postmarked on my birthday. It was a card from Eve with the caption in Italian, "St. Augustine leaves Rome for Milan." Italy, my old home, how ironic. She wrote:

A day towards the end of July.

> *Dear Nicki & I missed your b-day but I remembered it & when I am back in London I will send a book—a favorite book I urge all with romantic disposition to read plus a garment to withstand the rigors of a Washington winter. (I see you looking good in brown and it would be typically English.)*
>
> *Meanwhile summer in Tuscany; Looking at paintings, staying in the country not too far from the divine Firenze & enjoying heat & wine & Italians. We shall go slowly in our "relationship," I think, it may enrich (i.e., make more interesting!) our lives. If I am in U.S. soon, I would, be sure, be in touch with you.*

Love, Eve

Her tone was arty and reserved at the same time. I felt both seduced and disheartened. She was motherly but detached. I was almost clothed by her promise of dressing me in a warm brown jacket. Never mind that she never sent it. For now the promise of her affection, doled out in postcard-sized portions, was enough.

Shortly thereafter, a slim package arrived bearing Eve's spidery scrawl. No jacket, but a book, wrapped in utilitarian brown paper. It was *Le Grand Meaulnes* (*The Wanderer*) by Alain Fornier. I'd never heard of it. A card was tucked into the cover page. It was a postcard of a Picasso painting, showing a nude boy giving a smaller boy a piggyback ride. It was called "Les Deux Freres."

Not a card of a mother and daughter but two brothers. How odd.
I wanted to believe in my mother, not this mystery woman, but
again I tucked my doubts under like hospital corners and
breathed life into her threadbare affection. She would love me,
she would come around. It had always been a waiting game, I
told myself. I must be patient and continue to wait for the out-
pouring of love I didn't want to admit I had expected.

Both Philip and Eve chided me for not finding them earlier. He
had written "I wish you'd made yourself known to me years ago"
and she wrote, "If you haven't [read this book]—you should have
done. . . ." I marveled over their statements, innocent, certainly,
but thoughtless. Where were *they* that they didn't make themselves known to *me*? And who was there to advise me on books I
should have read when I was "17 or thereabouts"? I tried not to be
oversensitive but wasn't always successful. Doubts and dreams
and hopes plagued and enchanted me; after a while, there was no
one to share them with. Even my boyfriend Jim and my friends
tired of hearing how I scrutinized postcards and cancelled stamps
for meaning. I'm sure I'd become a complete bore. My family
seemed defensive about anything beyond generalities on the subject of the search.

By that winter, I had received three cards from Eve, always
written impatiently, as if she never had time to draft a full-fledged

letter, as if she were too busy to think of me, too busy to cope, too busy going to the movies, the theater, and art openings to feel me waiting. Perhaps she was so busy *because* she felt me waiting. Despite my anxiety and her reticence, her cards delighted me and I treasured them as I learned the shape and texture of her personality. She was passionate about art and fiercely independent, qualities I identified with. Yet fiercely she held back her heart. Would not tell her husband about me. Would not tell her family. She was afraid, I believed, that if she told her husband she would lose her security; after all, she had never worked or supported herself. Her resistance to telling him bespoke fear and dependence. I wanted to give her time, so I waited like a stone.

Philip's wife sent me a Christmas card that year: "Dear Nicki, I keep reading your correspondence with Philip so I thought I'd better introduce myself ." Averill was warm and cheerful and wrote about their dogs, horses, cats, and extended family. She also invited me to come and visit soon. But I didn't, I couldn't. I was still waiting for Eve.

The next year, 1985, brought big changes in my life. I was offered a position at another government agency as a writer-editor, working for a playwright friend. Years ago, when I had met Terryl at my writer's group, I asked her how she made a living. I always asked playwrights how they made a living; so few of us can make a living from our plays, we need good day jobs. She explained that she managed a group of writers at an agency whose name sounded like "The Dusty Depository of Tedious Insurance." I practically nodded off as she was reciting the name of the place.

Imagine my surprise several years later to find myself employed by the same quasi-government agency, the Federal Deposit Insurance Corporation. If everything worked out well, I would get promoted each year until I reach the position of Senior Writer, which had a lovely ring. Shortly after I took the job, Jim's roommate moved from the house he rented in Northwest

Washington and Jim invited me to move in with him. Some people accept change easily, but I wasn't one of them. I agonized over the decision. We had a good relationship as it was. I had a cozy downtown apartment from which I walked to work. After tortured contemplation and consultation with friends, I took the plunge and move uptown.

Jim helped create a study out of the recently-vacated room and I was reassured to see my computer and desk set up, fresh paint on the walls. My first evening living there, I silently mourned the loss of privacy. I'll never be able to brush my teeth alone again, I thought. A voice in my head advised me to shut the bathroom door. I did, and things worked out fine.

Philip professed to hate writing letters, which as a writer, I found incomprehensible, but he tried. I was always pleased to see his handwriting on the envelope and the familiar "M." A recent letter had alarmed me, written on the stationery of the Park Hospital, Nottingham:

Dear Nicki,

> *You can see that I am in hospital. I have had an operation to remove a displaced disk in my back but don't worry, the surgeon said it was successful and I will be back to normal within the next two months if I take it easy!*

Mortality tapped on the window once again. I released the breath I'd caught. I wasn't ready to lose him yet.

> *You don't have to start making quick replies because I've been unwell. I am OK so just let me hear from you in your own good time. (That doesn't mean I don't want to hear from you!) I do hope you decide to visit the UK this year. We are all looking forward to having you stay with us.*

As I read this, I knew I was not ready to go to England yet. Not until Eve. . .

> *. . . I was so happy that you found me. It doesn't matter that you were an accident of birth, you are a fact and part of me, and although I've only been with you a few hours, I love you accordingly, so make the effort to give us a chance to get to know each other. My children are young enough to be told you were a daughter of a previous marriage long forgotten. Rochelle [the daughter of his first marriage] is old enough to be told the same thing.*
>
> *Good night, God bless sweet child,*
> *Philip XXXX*

His words reassured me that I was wanted after all, which I'd doubted. Yet, I didn't want to visit England if I couldn't see Eve. I didn't want to confront or expose her. I never wanted to hurt her. Though I longed to visit Philip's family, which would welcome me, I couldn't yet accept that Eve would never do the same. Consequently, Britain became a zone of reckoning I was afraid to enter. The more Philip invited, the harder it became to accept Eve's rejection. I put myself on hold, waiting for her to change her mind; and I'd never liked waiting.

Chapter 9

After a regular check up in 1985, the doctor said I had a pre-cancerous condition requiring hospitalization and a biopsy. General anesthesia. Overnight stay. Surgery. I was a mass of alarm, talked to too many people, and in an effort to comfort myself, sought out a women's medical guide in which my operation was discussed; from the illustrations, it looked as if they were going to remove a piece of me the size of a peach. Blessed with a strong constitution, I was the typical case of a person who'd never thought much about her health until she might be losing it. Even after the doctor explained that what she'd excise would be the size of my little fingernail, I worried.

I worried too about my mother, Moo. For months, no one had heard from her. When I did get a letter, her handwriting was almost unreadable from arthritis. A cousin of my father's wrote and said he'd met her accidentally on the street in Norwich. He was sorry to report she was in a terrible way, incoherent from drink and defenseless against people who might exploit her. Of course she had no telephone. "Why don't you call your father," suggested Jim. "He's closer than we are, and he might know someone nearby."

I wrote to Daddy who was living and working in Germany. By calling my mother's neighbor, he discovered Moo had recently received a small inheritance from the family of an old friend and was on a bender. After I had recuperated from the operation, I called the Salvation Army in Norwich to ask if they would investigate Moo's situation. They said they would send someone around to her flat. I was tempted to visit but apprehensive of what I might find. Daddy sent her money occasionally, but she was essentially adrift in the world and had been for years. I was torn between trying to save her from herself and knowing that I couldn't.

Major Duncan with the Salvation Army reported that he'd talked to Moo after several tries. He said there were some other people at the flat, "shady types," he opined, but she said she was fine and that they were her friends. She told him to tell me to write to her, that she missed my letters. Moo and I had always been avid correspondents. I hadn't written to her of late mostly because I was angry that she seemed bent on destroying herself. I'd selectively applied the childhood teaching that if you don't have anything nice to say, don't say anything at all. Now I could see how my silence had hurt her. The truth was she was ill and couldn't help herself and my being angry was an unkind blow.

I composed a letter, striking the right balance, I hoped, between acceptance and honesty, love and detachment. I laughed as I reworked the letter: No matter which mother I wrote to, I had to choose my words carefully. Gone were the carefree days of corresponding: "Dear Moo, Let me tell you all about what I am doing. . ." Perhaps those days were like the Golden Age of Radio, real but short-lived when you stopped to count the years.

By this time, Moo and I had lived most of our lives far apart, communicating by airmail. I was learning to do it again with Eve. A face-to-face relationship with a mother would have astounded me, which was not to say that a relationship by mail was not rewarding, but it was a series of monologues, not a dialogue. It's hard to have an argument by mail or an embrace. Still, we'd learned to make do with our distances.

I chose a cheerful card to send, a reproduction of a Matisse painting called "The Purple Robe." A woman in a flowing robe sat leaning on her elbow in a colorful room with flowers and a plate of oranges and mangoes next to her.

March 20, 1986

Dear Moo,

Just a note to wish you happy Easter on this, the first day of spring. Jim and I are both fine and happy that winter's over. The crokes and daffodils are starting to come up in the garden. I haven't heard from you in ever so long a time, and both Daddy and I are concerned.

I know what's happening, that you got the money from your Uncle (Daddy talked to your neighbor to find out if you were all right because we've been out of touch). I can't help wishing that you'd used some of it to come and visit us. I accept that you are doing what you feel you need to do, and though I don't like it, I will always love you very much.

My new one act play, Starman, Wish Me Luck, *is out at several theaters for consideration. It's sort of about you. Also I expect to get promoted next month, having been here a year and doing well. Please write when you're able.*

Love,
Nicki X

Easter Sunday was early that year, March 30. I got up with the sun and went for a ride on a friend's horse. Such a pleasure, being out in the woods with an old racing thoroughbred, the songbirds in full throat, a fresh green world come to life again. On the way home, I stopped at the drugstore to buy Jim some Easter candy. It was a tradition with us, that one or the other would wait till Easter Day and get the eggs half price. I pulled up at the house and began unloading saddle, boots, and paraphernalia. Jim came out of the house to greet me. "What a fabulous ride," I said.

"Nicki, I've got bad news." Do we only call our loved ones by name when there's something wrong? I saw his face and I knew. "It's your Mom. I'm afraid she's dead. The hospital in Norwich called. She had a heart attack last night."

Jim hugged me as I stood in the front yard crying. I'd known this was coming, but I was not prepared to lose her forever. I called the hospital and eventually reached the doctor who had admitted her. She'd collapsed at her flat and was brought to the hospital unconscious. In the middle of the night, she'd had a heart attack and died, without much suffering, he said. I walked around the house in a daze.

"Stay home from work," said Jim. "I'll call your office. They won't expect you in; you're in no shape to work." He always seemed to know the right thing to do. In the quiet of Monday afternoon, lying in a hammock in the back yard, I stared into the pink blossoms of the flowering plum tree, taking in the shape of my altered world. It was a beautiful day; I was wearing shorts and a T-shirt on March 31. Yet on this very same day, my mother lay dead. There was so much we hadn't done and would never do now. Regret capsized me, but I held to the knowledge that in my last words, received a few days before her death, I'd told her I loved her and had ceased passing judgment. I was grateful for that. Our fierce love for each other had endured decades of separation but now in grief

I couldn't understand why. Pink blossoms against a blue sky; I couldn't fathom it.

Because I was the child who had been closest to Moo, burial arrangements came down to me. I knew she didn't want to be cremated; she'd told me repeatedly how traumatic her own mother's cremation had been. "What should I do?" I asked Jim. He'd handled his mother's death arrangements a few years before I'd met him. "Italy? Norwich? Here?" I thought about my heritage, too, but it wasn't as if Moo were Jewish and had to be buried the next day. The doctor had assured me there was no hurry.

"Pick someplace you think you'll visit. Why not Nottingham?" said Jim. I called Daddy and we decided on Nottingham. It was where Moo and I were born, where she was raised, and where she'd met my father, and because Philip lived there, I privately expected to be returning to visit.

I called the hospital and told the doctor our plans. "By the way," I asked him, "how did you get my telephone number to notify me?" Daddy had asked and I didn't know. "It was in your Mum's handbag," said the doctor. "At least your address was. On the Easter card you sent her. She had it with her."

Jim and I flew over and met Daddy in Norwich to clean out Moo's flat and settle her affairs. We packed up the old photographs and mementos, but there wasn't much left. I reluctantly locked her apartment for the last time but when we got back to our hotel, I sobbed because I hadn't stayed longer, kept more of her threadbare possessions. Jim was comforting. He'd also lost his mother to alcoholism. We both knew that I was really crying about the finality and pity of it all. Later that afternoon, Daddy went to the bank and closed her account. Someone had cleaned out the money that was left using an ATM card, but there was nothing to be done. When it was over, Daddy, Jim and I drove to Nottingham for the funeral. Neither my brother nor sister came, predictable given that they'd been estranged from Moo for years. I was the only one who hadn't let go.

The process of burying her was draining but being there helped me remember the warmth we'd shared: her rapt attention as she watched my riding lessons; holding her hand when as a five-year-old she and I had walked into the splendor of Covent Garden to see Nureyev and Fontaine dance; our kitchen talks; our walks and market investigations; the letters she sent me at boarding school, signed with her scrawl and my new puppy's paw print; the special salads she made me after school when I was a plump teenager frustrated with gaining weight; our soup and Marmite sandwich lunches, and walking into Philip's store with her arm snugly though mine.

My siblings had let go of sharing her difficult life. I had insisted and squeezed out every experience our relationship could support, even as her grip on sanity grew weak. On my last trip, when Moo and I had journeyed to Nottingham to find Philip, I'd scrubbed her bathroom floor, stocked her kitchen, and washed her clothes and linens. I'd put up with her pub friends, her incontinence, and the specter of her ravaged face. In the end, even with the difficulties, I was grateful to have been there for her as she had been there for me.

We buried her on a breezy slope in Sherwood with a bundle of fragrant dried roses and a copy of the play I'd written for her. My office colleagues sent a big spray of flowers. I sat between Jim and Daddy and cried on my father's shoulder as the priest intoned his blessings in the cold chapel. Although Gerrie had died of cancer a few years before, Moo's remaining old friends, Rosemary and Anne, attended with us, and we went back to Rosemary's house after the funeral for tea.

Daddy, Jim, and I were staying at a hotel in downtown Nottingham. Before I'd left, I'd written to Philip and Eve, letting them know I would be here and would like to see them. Some months before, Eve had written me an ambiguous note implying I could begin writing to her at home if I didn't do it too often. Building a relationship with her was like befriending a wild animal. It had been almost two years since we met. My patience seemed to be paying off; her tentative move encouraged me.

Because we were in England for Moo's funeral, I didn't want to tell Daddy I was meeting Philip. It seemed in bad taste to choose this trip to introduce them or for Jim and me to go off and meet Philip's family, leaving Daddy alone. Yet taking him along for my first visit with his family seemed unthinkable. Jim agreed. Looking back, I probably should have pushed through the awkwardness and seized the moment but I didn't. Instead, I invited Philip over to the hotel for a drink while Daddy took a nap. Without realizing it, I was falling into Eve's intrigue. When Philip arrived, I introduced him to Jim, and we ordered drinks in the hotel lounge.

"A dark beer, please," said Jim, unused to English drinking customs. When served what looked like a gallon of Guinness stout, he bravely said nothing. To support the cause, he drank as much as he could while keeping a watchful eye out for Daddy. Philip and I chatted about the economy, his business, and our lives and eventually got around to the subject of us.

"You know," Philip said, "I knew exactly who you were when you called me the first time."

"You did?" I asked.

"I'm afraid I had buried it very deeply in my mind, but I knew."

"It was a very long time ago," said Jim.

Philip nodded his head. He talked about his first marriage and subsequent divorce. "I had this idea, and my mother did, that I ought to marry a Jewish girl. And Eve and I had already broken up months before. But my marriage was a disaster. Looking back on it, I could have done a lot worse than marry Eve. We probably would have been quite happy. Will you be seeing her in London?"

"I'd like to," I said. I hadn't called Eve, and she hadn't followed up on my letter. I felt ashamed she wouldn't see me, as if there were something wrong with me.

Philip was disappointed we wouldn't come out to the house and meet Averill and the kids. Although he respected my decision, I didn't think he appreciated the nuances of the situation. I did want to meet his family, but Daddy had already planned to drive us back to London the next day. I couldn't abandon him as if his only usefulness—helping me bury Moo—were over and my feelings were the only ones that counted. An hour in a dark hotel bar was not the ideal reunion follow-up but it was all I could manage. When we said goodbye, it was with both pleasure and regret. Some decisions are never satisfying no matter how right they may be.

After dispatching Philip, I dragged a semi-drunken Jim up to our room to freshen up. It was almost time for us to meet Daddy and Anne for more drinks and dinner in the rooftop restaurant. Whoever thought the mystery disappeared when the search was over had a few things to learn about mine. Jim and I stumbled through dinner and collapsed in our room when it was over, laughing, somewhat tipsy, feeling like spies.

Back in London, Daddy and Jim returned to the States, and I stayed on a few days with Fiona, catching up and hoping to see Eve. I was lying on the floor in the guestroom doing yoga when the phone rang. It was Eve. "Yes, I imagine you're very health conscious," she said to me when she asked what I was doing. "No, I'm afraid I couldn't possibly see you at the moment," she said in her bitingly upper class tone. "I have a daughter going back to Oxford and I'm terribly busy." With what, I thought, ironing her button-down shirts?

"Of course, I understand," I said. To not be understanding would only rain trouble down on my head but I was achingly disappointed, and later, angry. Of course Eve wouldn't see me, coming as I was from Moo's funeral. It might be too involving. While she chattered about art and theater and Greece, she pushed me away with both hands. A month later, she sent me an envelope full of photocopies of her drawings and a card, a Royal Shakespeare Company photo of Viola and Orsino from *Twelfth Night,* sweet and romantic. She knew how to ring my bell.

Dearest Nicki,

I send you a few print outs of my wiggly line drawings, most from around Regents Park, down the road or Southwold. You sound good. I think of you with affection.

Yours,
Eve

One day I will write a letter!

By sending me evidence of her artistic self, I reasoned that she was trying to bridge the gap created by refusing to see me. I saw a pattern emerge of push pull. After a decent interval, I wrote back, thanking her for the drawings. I told her I had written my adoption search story as a Toastmasters speech (with names changed, of course) and offered her an opportunity to read it. A response arrived quickly.

Dear Nicki,

Thanks v. much for your letter. Briefly, I like you but I cannot help but resent (not quite the right word) the 'intrusion' into my privacy, by your investigation—except I understand completely your need to search, & hopefully discover. I would not like to read of that search.

Love,
Eve

"She sure likes to play yo-yo, doesn't she," said Jim, after he read her letter. "And you're on the end of the string." The boundary she set was severe: Never talk about the past. My search story was dramatic but I thought it had a happy ending. What pain was she afraid I'd unearth? Just as our relationship was warming and trust was building, she turned away like a petulant child, went into her room, and slammed the door. I had second thoughts about wanting her as a mother.

"At least you didn't have to grow up with that craziness," said Jim. I decided I wouldn't write to her for a while. She didn't write to me either, but she'd always been able to best me in the surprise department. If Eve's latest response sent me spinning, the next letter to arrive from England was a real knock-out.

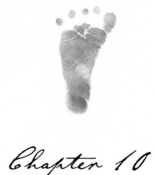

Chapter 10

Farragut North Metro Station. The circular lights embedded in the granite platform pulsed, heralding a train. I was on my way home from work in September 1986. Like a bubble rising to the sea's surface, a thought came to my mind: I wonder if I'll ever meet Eve's daughters, my sisters. Stepping onto the train, I mused, yes, but perhaps not for a long time.

Ten days later, I opened the front door and found the mail stacked neatly on the stairs. Jim was already home from his new job as production manager of *Science* magazine, taking a pre-dinner nap. The house was quiet. Beneath a bill and a bank statement lay a large white envelope addressed in an energetic hand, displaying blue airmail stickers. It wasn't from Eve or Philip or Fiona. I turned it over and read the return address: Angela Saddler, 44 Howard Place, Hampstead, London NW3, UK. I tore it open and read:

September 26th

Dear Nicki,

Who the hell is this letter from, you are thinking! Yes, I know, it's all very bizarre, but I am Angela, your half-sister and this situation is one that occurs in soap operas, not real life. . .

. . . I think Mum decided to share her secret with me, partly because my parental situation is also rather strange and partly because I am seriously considering immigrating to the States. . . .

She'd enclosed a photograph, penetrating eyes and dangling earrings, the kind I might wear, wavy hair like mine but blonde, and a very familiar face. I rushed to waken Jim. "Look," I said, pushing the photo in front of his sleepy face. "Who does this remind you of?"

I ran to the kitchen to make him coffee, to wake him up to appreciate the enormity of what had happened. All evening long, we reread the letter. I took the picture into my office and asked my colleagues pointedly, "Who is this?" "Who does this remind you of?" Most of the time, people stared at the picture, looked at me, and said, "Your sister?" For an adoptee, this was a sublime moment: to look like someone for the world to see, to be related to someone after all. In her letter, Angela began to tell me her story:

I was the product of a long love affair between Mum and a professor. After she became pregnant with me, he left her to marry another woman and she met and married Thomas when I was five. I have two other half-sisters Marianne and Jules, who are eighteen and sixteen respectively.

Needless to say, Mum is very secretive about her past and never discusses it. I'm the only person to know of your exis-

tence and I think she wants it kept that way. Maybe one day my sisters will be able to share the secret too—it would intrigue them.

It's strange that you, too, should 'discover' your real parents. Mum always refused to divulge the truth about my real father and I was forced to adopt the pose of an undercover detective. I was amazed to discover that he was the university president, living about a mile away from our house! I've never met him; I do not want to disrupt his life and he, equally, has done nothing for me.

I don't want you to feel that I'm intruding in your life. You must be honest with me about that. . . .

Intruding? I'd had my fill of enforced privacy. I was more than ready to be involved with my sister Angela, the one who writes. She continued:

Let's see, I'm 23 (two days ago), 5 foot 3 inches tall, blondish with green eyes. No, I'll stop this—it's starting to sound like an advert in the Lonely Hearts column. I'll enclose a photo instead.

I've just graduated from London University in Modern Languages (French and German) and am looking for a decent job. It's not easy with 3 million unemployed and this being such a small island in the ocean, but I am persevering and living on social security for the time being. I'm trying for all the oversubscribed careers in T.V., video, music, etc., and my confidence regularly takes a bash! Having done a lot of freelance work, you must appreciate what it's like.

I am very interested to know how and why you decided to live in the States. At the ripe old age of 23 I feel that England is just not for me. My long standing boyfriend of 4 1/2 years (Jack) and I have decided to save up as much money as possible, over about 18 months, and then come to America and tour around

for a while, then maybe, if possible, get jobs. It's been a dream
we have shared ever since we first met. Perhaps you could give
me some tips on the entry procedure, because after all, you are
English, aren't you?

I hope you don't resent this bold intrusion, but I just felt I
had to write. Look forward to hearing from you.

Love, Angela

Resentment was the last thing on my mind. I was delighted to
be wanted, sought after, and found and I wrote back immediately. Eve never said a word.

Angela and I began a spirited correspondence across the Atlantic. I bounded home to check the mail every evening. Two
weeks after sending my first letter to her, a reply arrived:

October 23, 1986

Dear Nicki,

Many thanks for your letter and photos. You are the spitting
image of Mum! It's strange that out of all us girls you resemble
her the most. Perhaps I should explain the enclosed photo of
Mum. I thought you might appreciate a picture of her in her
younger days, not that there are many of them (she's very se-
cretive about her past). The resemblance to you is striking.

We're determined to save hard before coming over to the
States. We are thinking of buying a van in America, so that
we can cruise around and see as much of the country as pos-
sible without paying for expensive accommodations. Do you
think that would be a good idea? Apparently, when one ap-
plies for a visa over there, the length of time you're given is

mainly dependent on the amount of money you prove to have in your possession.

It's really winter. England is getting colder all the time. The leaves lie in a slushy mess on the pavement, the wind blows and the rain falls. I wouldn't miss this climate, I can promise you that! We have a little cottage on the East Coast (where Mum and I lived before she married Thomas) and it's a lovely getaway. It's a pretty little seaside town and blissfully quiet in the winter—just the thing to contrast with the eternal rat-race in London.

Cross-country skiing sounds lovely! I did go skiing once with some friends in the Italian Dolomites, but I somehow managed to dislocate my hip on a downhill slope, which has made me slightly nervous about taking it up again. Cross-country sounds just up my street. As you said, there is no such thing as coincidence and I am a great believer in Fate. I am so happy our paths have crossed at last. Jack sends his love—he is just as excited as I am about you. Write soon,

Love, Angela

Every letter from Angela was a window into Eve's life and the new reality that I shared not only appearances with my blood kin but habits, tones, and tendencies. I'd long held to the 'Nurture over Nature' school of thinking because I had no nature to refer to. In Angela's voice, I heard responses to the calls I'd made as a child into the boundless night. Like cries across a summer lake—"Hello?"—with nothing but the song of frogs and crickets as reply until one night a voice cried back—Hello!" faint but real, a mysterious mingling of language and blood.

A few months later, I was getting dressed for work and the radio was on. For my previous birthday, Daddy had given me a portable short wave/FM radio. Having grown up listening to radio rather than watching TV, I listened to the news in the morning, talk shows in the evening, and radio documentaries on Saturday morning. I listened doing the dishes, taking a bath, brushing my teeth. I was a radio girl, I couldn't help it. "Morning Edition" was on and I overheard a story about an immigration lottery. Visitors could send in applications for a chance to win a Green Card, the document giving immigrants the right to work here and eventually become citizens.

The announcer gave sketchy details about applications being available at the State Department. I mentioned the story to Grace, one of my colleagues. She was married to an Englishman and they had been trying to get her brother-in-law an opportunity to immigrate for years. The process was slow, even if you had a relative here. Immediately, Grace insisted we race over to the State Department to pick up applications. It seemed a curious way of doing business. The State Department itself didn't seem to know what was going on.

I'd already looked into the possibility of sponsoring Angela for immigration. After only letters and occasional phone calls, we already felt like sisters. The lottery might be my chance to help her. Grace's brother-in-law had been on the immigration list for over four years and had barely moved up.

I discovered that Congress had passed a law to redress the immigration imbalance resulting from the post-Vietnam War period. People from non-Asian countries would be given preference. All we had to do was submit the person's name, birth date and place, and home address. The tricky part was hitting the deadline correctly. Applications would be processed on a first-come, first-served basis. A person could apply as many times as he liked, but any applications arriving *before* the deadline would be discarded. My office mates volunteered to mail applications for Grace and me at their local post offices in Virginia, Maryland, and the District. I typed up dozens of applications each for Jack and Angela. Two days before the date, I mailed them at four different post offices and listened for news stories about the lottery but the media was quiet. The first week in March, I got a letter from Angela:

Dear Nicki,

I'm so sorry about the delay in writing, but life has been abnormally hectic and I never seem to have time to myself. Every day I say, `I'll get that letter done today' and every day passes, you know the feeling.

I have finally landed a 'proper' job in shipping. Having almost reached the end of my tether and an all-time confidence low, I was offered about four jobs in one week. I chose this one because of the opportunity to use my languages, the interest factor, and of course, the money, which is pretty reasonable for a graduate with no experience. I am a trainee area coordinator (France) and the job is very diverse. The company is called Trans Ocean Ltd. and is in fact American, which may prove to be useful. Our headquarters are in San Bruno, near San Francisco, which can't be bad. I think I will like it, but at the moment, it's hard work and chaotic. My parents are naturally thrilled to have me out of the house five days a week and already I'm wondering where my social life has gone.

The latest news is that both Jack and I have received notification from the U.S. embassy in London of our applications. This does not necessarily mean, of course, that we will get immigration visas but it is a step forward. There is naturally a series of procedures to follow, starting with a 'who are you and where do you live' type of form. From there, we have to trace such things as birth certificates with two parents on it.

I have a problem there, since I only have my mother's name on the certificate. Anyway, to support the application, there are 'Affidavit of Support' forms and I have enclosed them in

the presumption that you might be our 'support.' Of course,
that is purely for the red tape, I assure you, I don't want you
thinking we want to be dependent on you. In any case, if you
feel like filling them in, the address to send them follows. . . .

I completed the forms and called the State Department. They told me that applications were being completed by all the eligible applicants. In May, Angela wrote:

The U.S. embassy has contacted me re: an interview and
said that they would be sending a time and date soon. You also
have to have a medical examination, supply X million docu-
ments and pay about £150, so it is serious stuff.

"Does this mean she won the lottery?" I asked Jim. We reread her letter.

"She didn't mention it," he said, "but you never mailed the regular immigration form." It dawned on us belatedly that Angela had actually won a Green Card in the lottery. She would be coming soon.

The embassy had told her that proof of our relationship and my co-sponsorship would help her application. I documented that we were sisters, got a letter from my supervisor certifying my job and salary, and sent an affidavit stating I would support her if it came to that. In June, she wrote:

Dear Nicki,

A peaceful few minutes at work so I thought at last I would
drop you a line. I had my 'day out' (including full medical) at
the U. S. Embassy and it all went very smoothly. Everything
has been approved, they say, and I will get my papers as soon

as my passport has been renewed. I was very pleased and it was all down to you. And without the support papers, it would have been a lot tougher. They didn't ask me any awkward questions and were very friendly and helpful—quite the best bureaucratic organization I have ever encountered.

Realizing that Jack and I had planned to travel together, they were very sympathetic, but said that he would not receive his interview date until the next 'batch' (whenever that was). They also mentioned that we could always get married once I had got my papers and that would be an easy way in for him. The law to keep the visa is that you have to make your first trip to the States within four months, so if I get my papers sometime next month (British bureaucracy permitting—the passport people are involved in a dispute), Jack and I shall pop over for a mini-break October time. I'll keep you informed— I haven't even got my visa yet. Jumping the gun as usual.

I expect by now you and Jim will be engaged. Congratulations! Save a place for me among the bridesmaids.

We lined up a job offer in a friend's home construction business for Jack. Angela said she would come anyway, but I knew she wanted Jack to come too. Our letters sped back and forth across the Atlantic as we discovered interests in common, especially writing. Though we hadn't even met, we were like old friends.

Eve kept her distance. She sent postcards that she tucked into gift books but ignored my growing relationship with Angela. I didn't really care. My work was going well, I was engaged to marry a sweet man, and my latest play would have a staged reading two days before my new sister's arrival.

Chapter 11

October 1987, Angela and Jack flew in on Continental Airlines. I called the airline every hour to check on their flight status and went home early in the afternoon to prepare to collect them from National Airport. When I got home, I called again and discovered their connection from New York to Washington was delayed. I tidied the house again and flipped through a magazine. How could I think of anything else?

Jim came home from work, and we called again. Their flight still hadn't left New York. We ate dinner. The airline relayed a message from Angela, confirming their delay in New York. At ten o'clock, Jim went to bed and said to wake him when it was time to leave. The airline called to say the plane had left New York but would be landing at Dulles Airport, miles away in Virginia. "Don't worry. We'll put all the passengers on a bus and drive them to National Airport," the clerk said. Just what they had been looking forward to when they landed—a bus ride.

It was past midnight when we pulled into the visitors parking lot at the airport, which was closed. A few passengers loitered in the shadow of the old art deco terminal, waiting to be collected. Even the taxis had abandoned their stand. I thought I could make out a man and a woman with a big suitcase but it was dark and their coats were drawn tightly around them. In one motion, Jim strode in their direction and boomed in a mock-English accent, "Are you English?" I cringed. He sounded like David Niven, a white *bwana* calling to jungle-weary compatriots from his colonial outpost in darkest Africa. His words echoed in the arches of the terminal but a voice replied emphatically, "Yes!"

After a twelve-hour journey, Angela and Jack had joyfully arrived at their destination, us. Jim helped them with their bag and told jokes. Jack whipped out a camera and memorialized the occasion. In the photo, both Angela and I are beaming. And we're both wearing red sweaters and gray jackets.

In the morning, I made coffee and waited for them to appear. Eventually they stumbled downstairs, and I filled their coffee cups and served breakfast. Angela looked out of the dining room window onto the park across the street. "It's quiet here, isn't it? Not what you'd imagine when you think of Washington, D.C., capital of the United States." She said 'United States' with a Yankee twang.

I told her Washington was full of tucked-away neighborhoods. "There's even a stable around the corner. We can take a walk up there when you're ready."

"I'll take some more coffee first then we'd love to," she said. I longed to ask what it was like growing up with Eve but took my cues from them to see how the conversation would develop. In their presence, my British reserve came to the surface. The American side of me cried out to ask, "What does Eve think about your visit?" When I could stand it no longer, I asked, "Who does your father think you're visiting? And how does he think you got papers?"

Angela gave a Mona Lisa smile. Don't hold back on me, I thought. "We told him about the lottery," she said. "Made it sound like we sent in an entry and, lucky bugs, got picked. I told him I was visiting a friend of Mum's."

"Thomas isn't very curious," said Jack. "Eve's always doing odd things he can't keep track of, out to a theater opening, jetting off to Italy. He's used to being in the dark is her dad."

I pushed forward. "What was it like growing up in your family?" I asked.

Angela contemplated the question. "Normal type of family," she said. "It didn't start that way. It was hard in the beginning, just me and Mum. I was only five when she met Thomas. When they married, I was indignant I had to stay with my Nana while they went on their honeymoon." She laughed. "I wasn't used to sharing her, but I soon adjusted. First Marianne, then Jules was born. I loved having little sisters. I was old enough not to feel jealous."

I asked her where she went to school. "We moved to Kent after my sisters were born. My Dad commuted on the train into London. It must have been hard. He got home quite late; I wouldn't see him for days. I went to a superb boarding school run by the Friends, the Quakers," she said. I told her my father and brother had been to Friends schools.

"Really? Where did you go?" she asked.

"I went to Cedar House near Cambridge, then The Grove in Hindhead, near Guildford."

"I know where The Grove is. We have friends who live near there. That's a very nice school."

"I liked it," I said. "What was Eve like as a mother?" I'd asked the question before I could stop myself.

Angela frowned. "Unusual, as you can imagine. She was fun, arty, but not. . ." She searched for the right words. ". . . not cuddly. I mean, she was. . ." Angela stopped, cautious but trying to be truthful. Jack interrupted.

"She's more interested in herself," he said. "I don't know what she was like when you were kids, but since I've known her, she's been wrapped up in her own stuff. She'll make you a cup of coffee but you have to fix your own sandwich."

"Not like your Mum," said Angela, smiling at Jack. "She feeds you from the moment you walk in the door. 'Have a biscuit? Cuppa tea? I've got some nice shrimp spread, what about a sandwich?'" Jack looked embarrassed.

"Spoil you rotten would my Mum," he said. He was an East Londoner, lean and pale. He spoke with such a thick Cockney accent that even I had difficulty deciphering. After looking around the kitchen, he'd asked "You on an 'elf kick?" I pictured tiny green dancers in a chorus line.

"Beg your pardon?" I asked.

"You and Jim on an 'elf kick? All I seen is lettuce an' tofu in the 'fridge."

"They're vegetarians," said Angela. Jack looked worried.

"Health kick. Got it. We're healthy eaters, you might say. But I'll take you to the grocery store. We can pick up whatever you'd like to eat."

"Ooh! I'd like to visit an American grocery store. We can get some steak," said Angela.

"Only if Nicki doesn't mind," Jack said.

"Don't mind a bit. I won't eat it but you should enjoy yourselves," I said.

"Great," said Angela, getting up and stretching. "Shall we take our walk up to the horses then go to the grocery store? That should be enough excitement for one day."

We strolled to Rock Creek Park Stables. Washington was showing off with Indian summer weather. "You rode as a girl, didn't you?" I asked.

"I was very horsy," she said. "Were you?"

"Madly," I said. On the way back from the stables, Jack took pictures of Angela and me, arms around each other, basking in the autumn sun in the meadow. After freshening up, we drove to the Chevy Chase Safeway for a cultural experience. Up and down the aisles, Angela and Jack exclaimed over cookies, cereal, and the endless meat counter. Even though English supermarkets exist, an American grocery store remains the apex of Yankee abundance. At the check-out, Angela stuffed some large bills in my hand, which I declined and we had our first fight. She won.

With its majestic vistas and museums, Washington is a fabulous place to share when friends and relatives visit. I was magnanimous with its bounty as we went sightseeing up and down the Mall, as if it were all mine to share. My colleagues, a close group of writers, wanted to meet them; they'd been part of the Angela revelations from the start. "Is America what you expected?" asked Grace.

"It's better but look who my tour guide is. I still can't get over it. I look at her and it's like seeing Mum. Even her mannerisms. You've only spent an hour with Mum, haven't you?" I nodded.

Passing his hands in front of him with a flourish, Jack said, "There's this thing Nicki does with her hands. And the way she looks when she's thinking—look, she's doing it now!"

"That's exactly how Eve looks," said Angela. "It's really strange but wonderful."

"Did you ever have an inkling that Eve had another daughter?" asked Terry, my friend and supervisor.

"Not a clue," said Angela. "I'm used to her hiding things. Whenever I noticed her being secretive, abruptly ending a discussion, hiding letters, I'd chalk it up to other events. Grandad, Mum's father, was killed in a car crash when I was nine, and Marianne and Mum were in the car. After that, you could never mention a car accident to Mum. Forbidden topic."

"Why do you suppose she told you about Nicki?" asked Terry. I was grateful that she was asking the questions.

"It was one of those nights when secrets were told," said Angela. She looked at Jack who grimaced. "We'd had a fight. When I came home, Mum was still up. She prowls the house at night, reading, doing yoga. She made me a cup of tea and we sat at the kitchen table talking. I told her I was going to immigrate to the States even if I had to go alone. When I get an idea, I'm immovable," she said. I understood exactly what Angela was referring to and reflected on my own stubbornness. "Mum tried to talk me out of it. 'But you don't know anyone,' she said. 'I don't care,' I said, 'I'm going!'

"Mum took a deep breath and said, 'Perhaps you do know someone.' At first, I thought she was joking except that it was hard for her to tell. And she swore me to secrecy," said Angela. Everyone at the table was listening, riveted. Terry, a fellow playwright, tapped me on the arm. "You lucky girl," she said, "what material!"

I wanted to show Angela and Jack some of the countryside and drove them to Potomac, Maryland, resplendent in fall foliage, to visit my friends Dana and Guy. It was Guy who'd offered Jack a job at his construction company; Jack wanted to thank him in person. As Angela and Jack played a game of tennis on an old court at Guy's father's house, I took pictures.

"She's very like you," said Dana, with surprise. "I could walk in a room with a hundred strangers and pick her out as your sister."

"I wish she wasn't going back soon," I said. "We've sat up for hours talking but there's so much to catch up on. Letters aren't the same." We spent the afternoon watching Dana's kids play and throwing a ball for the big black Labrador. Our lovely day was only mildly jarred when Guy came home and reported that the stock market had had its worst day since the Depression, plunging five hundred points. That evening, Jim and I took them to a friend's house who was a magician. He kept floating dollar bills around Angela's head. At one point, she turned and said, "It does seem magical, doesn't it?"

I drove them to the airport the following day. In our last moments at the gate, I said, "I love you" and immediately felt foolish. English people don't talk that way. But I did.

"We'll be back for your wedding in February," Angela said. "We'll see you very soon, lots of love." I watched the plane taxi away, waving in case they could see me. I'd always wanted a close family and for a week, I'd had one. With Angela, we'd quickly gone from letters to phone calls to sleeping under the same roof. I'd have to be satisfied with correspondence. I wrote to Angela and in a couple of weeks was rewarded with a reply.

Dear Nicki,

I'm sorry I haven't written before but it has taken a long time to 'ground' in the U.K. and I'm just grabbing a few minutes at work in a peaceful period nearing end of play. Both Jack and I really enjoyed ourselves being with you and Jim. It was very special and strange.

Even after a week, I felt choked up at having to say goodbye, as if I'd known you all my life, which was, let's face it, how it should have been. You have opened up a whole new world for us, not only in America itself, but in the people around you. I very much approve of my brother-in-law to be.

We didn't want to come back! One thing we both remarked upon on the journey back was the positive spirit and enthusiasm that seems to permeate the air in the States. It was so refreshing. Our sights are firmly set on making a go of it there, to my mind, there is simply no alternative. England seems so drab and negative in comparison, but be sure I'm not blinded by a week's pleasure in Northwest Washington. I am sure we will learn a lot when we do our trip.

I haven't had a chance to speak to Mum yet, so your letter has not been delivered. I know she is dying to get me alone to find out all about it, but my Dad is always there. Never mind, he goes to college tomorrow night, so I'll pop round and see her.

Love,
Angela

I wanted Eve to know everything about me. Perhaps Angela's stories would reassure her, allow her to be warmer toward me. Even as I pursued a relationship with Angela, I still wanted Eve to claim me for herself and the world. As Eve watched Angela and me become friends, a triangle emerged. Now I had to consider how my actions would affect all of us.

We planned our wedding for Valentine's Day. Jim and I decided to invite all my family. Neither of us expected Eve or Philip to come, but I thought they might enjoy being invited. Certainly I enjoyed the fantasy that they might come but didn't dwell on making introductions; the likelihood of either of them attending was slim.

A week before Christmas, Eve sent me a copy of a treasured family cookbook, Claudia Roden's *New Book of Middle Eastern Food*. She wrote, on a postcard of a Goya painting,

---

Dear Nicki & Jim,

HAPPY CHRISTMAS & NEW YEAR

The best cookbook ever. Favourites with us are Mishmishiya & Orange & Almond Cake.

Love from Eve XX

The next day, another English letter arrived, a card and letter from Angela's grandmother Moira, her father's stepmother. Although Eve had insisted Angela not tell anyone, Angela said she *had* to tell Moira. They weren't blood relatives but they were dear to each other all the same.

"Your family's a font of abundance," remarked Jim when I showed him Moira's card. The web was untangling. Angela had spoken of Moira, her romances and tragedies, and her kindness, which I soon discovered for myself:

My dear Nicole,

Now that I have seen the lovely snaps that Angela took of you and Jim and your enchanting home, I feel I know you both already. I just wanted to wish you every happiness for the future and shall be longing to hear all about the wedding and see some photos from Angela.

Isn't it marvelous that you have "found" each other and love each other as sisters? I know what it is like as I had three sisters (sadly one died recently) and we have always been very close to each other, not only sisters but best friends.

On New Years Eve, Jim and I returned home and found our house had been burgled; jewelry and Jim's musical equipment were missing. This was scary and infuriating; Jim's band was playing at our wedding, and the burglars had stolen some of his keyboards. We slept wrapped in blankets on the living room floor, paring knives under our pillows and an overstuffed chair against the front door. I suppose if the burglars had returned, we'd have peeled them to death. A week before the wedding, Philip telephoned apologetically. "I'm sorry but I won't be able to attend. I hope you understand," he said.

"I do," I said. "I wanted to invite you though."

"Will you send photographs?" he asked. I assured him I would. "I wish you every happiness," he said. "Averill and I will be thinking of you. I hope you'll come and visit soon. God bless."

Two days to go and Angela and Jack arrived. Collecting them from the airport felt like old times. We stopped in the bar and toasted the official receipt of their Green Cards. When the guys went out to the recording studio to celebrate with Jim, Jack went with them, and Angela and I spent the evening together doing our hair.

"I think Mum might have lived in Greece when she was pregnant with you," said Angela as I turned off the hair dryer.

"Why do you say that?"

"Something she said recently. She worked as a maid in a hotel there. Then the Greek civil war broke out and the foreigners had to leave," said Angela.

"How romantic," I replied.

"Always," said Angela.

Did my love of olives and Mediterranean food come from pre-natal experience? "Where did she live in Greece?" I asked. "What happened when she came back to England?"

"I'm afraid I don't know anything else. She's discreet to the point of paranoia. She's not a bad mother but she's never been overly affectionate. She loves Greece; she glows when she's there. We've been dozens of times. It's her spiritual home, the food, the people," said Angela. I'd never been to Greece. I wished I could go there with her too.

Of course, Eve didn't attend the wedding but she sent me a pair of antique gold earrings and a card by way of Angela:

For Dear Nicki,

You were happy on your Wedding Day. May it last forever.

The earrings belonged to my mother & are Victorian. Love to Jim.

Love from Eve.

Angela gave me an inlaid wooden jewelry box that had also belonged to our grandmother. The blue satin lining must have witnessed countless parties and been the nest for many keepsakes. History, the satin lining of our lives, was enveloping me.

The night before the wedding was an insanity I'd planned without anyone's prodding. The whole wedding party, our families, and special guests were coming to our house for a buffet dinner.

That night, the house was packed with people. I introduced Angela to my adopted sister Chris and to Daddy. Thanks to the party atmosphere, there wasn't much opportunity to feel awkward. My sister Chris hated to fly and I appreciated the effort her being there represented. If she felt ill at ease meeting Angela, she didn't show it. Her more conventional life contrasted with my world of art, music, and flamboyant friends; perhaps my newfound sister was simply another unusual sight that weekend. As for Angela, she joked and chatted and was as charming as ever.

Our wedding was like a Broadway show that opened and closed on the same night. The Kennedy Warren Ballroom was abuzz as bridesmaids entered along the carpeted mezzanine, down the winding staircase, and through the crowd to the sound of hip-hop wedding music Jim had arranged for the occasion. Angela joined my other bridesmaids, Genni and Dana, on the stage. If my world didn't know about Angela before, they knew now. I wasn't only marrying, which I never thought I'd do. I was bringing together the disparate parts of my life: friends and relatives, American and English, arty and traditional. In the 1930s-era ballroom, decorated with blue and pink neon sculpture and tropical palms, brothers and sisters befriended each other. Jim's band played, and we ate, danced, and mingled the night away. Goodbye to Angela was different the second time around. I was certain soon she'd be back in the States for good. This time I was the one catching an airplane, and she was the one with house keys.

Chapter 12

ngela and Jack moved to the States in early summer. Their first residence was our guestroom. Angela found a job through a friend of mine who supervised the front desk clerks at the U.S. State Department. Jack got a job driving a truck for a local florist. Angela and I rode to work on the Metro and since her office was a quick walk from mine, we often lunched together. It was a fairy tale life. Usually I'd walk to her office, we'd eat in the cafeteria, and browse the Foreign Service Used Bookstore. Sometimes we'd picnic in the park. Once we walked through the Vietnam Veterans Memorial.

"So many names," she murmured as we walked down the path. The inscribed black granite wall reflected our faces. As we walked toward the center of the memorial, it gradually overwhelmed us as the war had overwhelmed the country. It rose above us until the grass grew over our heads like a grave. All around people milled, some lightly touching names on the wall, some searching for someone special, some like us just looking.

Children ran back and forth along the path. "I was confused about this war," said Angela.

"Join the club," I said.

"I was ten when it ended. I remember those cryptic reports on the television, Vietcong this and American that. The pictures of helicopters and people shooting at each other in the jungle. Mum used to change the channel. She doesn't like the intrusion of the real world. She never reads the front page of the paper; she goes straight to the Arts section."

"I was almost too young to understand," I said, "but I lived on a U.S. Air Force base from '69 to '71. G.I.s I knew from the base cafeteria would disappear on TDY, transfer of duty to Vietnam, and they never came back. The only English-language newspaper was the military *Stars and Stripes*. I couldn't get a sense of what was going on from that. I do remember the bombing of Cambodia after I was back in Massachusetts, watching Nixon on TV, lying through his teeth."

"I remember Nixon," she said, "what a strange fish he was."

In politics, our seven years' age difference determined how much of the explosive '60s and '70s we'd experienced. We shared books and learned each other's literary tastes. Having studied French literature, Angela introduced me to the works of Zola. She also loved the Americans John Steinbeck and Susanna Moore. I shared Athol Fugard, the Canadian Robertson Davies, and Alice Walker. I'd never exchanged books with my adopted sister.

After a few months of sharing living space, we also began to discover some of our differences. The guestroom where she and Jack were staying was also my study, and I yearned for my writing room back. Angela and Jack kept different hours and were not accustomed to the give-and-take of group house living; we had another roommate to consider. I began making polite noises about independence. Sensing it was time to find their own place, they rented a room in a house not far away in Maryland. We continued to see each other for lunch and on weekends, and they explored Washington on their own.

To many Europeans, America is still the frontier adventure-land revealed in movies and TV. Angela and Jack had seen the movie *Lost in America* and dreamed of buying a van and traveling the American byways and backwaters in search of authentic experiences. Their dream destination was New Orleans, harlot honky-tonk queen of the Mississippi. I recalled traveling across country in college and tempered my older sister wisdom with the gift of letting them discover America for themselves. Their roommate sold them an old Chevy van. The van's most notable characteristic was a hand-painted mural on the side that Jim described as "a naked winged blond man ascending into a red heaven." Thinking of them driving through Savannah, Jacksonville, and Baton Rouge, we bit our tongues hard.

They spent the rest of the summer fixing the van up. Jack dedicated himself to the mechanical repairs and Angela renovated the interior. In August, they quit their jobs and drove over to say farewell before embarking on their adventure. The plan was to drive down to the North Carolina beaches, continue south to Florida and west to New Orleans, where they hoped to find jobs and settle down. Once again, I was sorry to see Angela go. I wished she'd settle down the street, but she and Jack were electrified in anticipation of their expedition so I supplied surplus pots, pans, dishes, blankets, and bug spray and waved them on their way.

Weeks went by without a word. By then, I knew Angela well enough to understand that when life went well, she'd communicate regularly; when it didn't, nothing. Her behavior was a window into Eve's life. My yearning to be part of Eve's family subsided as I learned what it would really be like, a place where I couldn't speak my mind, where passions and fears were cloistered and ordinary subjects taboo. Sometimes I was glad not to have grown up there.

Jim and I went house-hunting. We liked our quiet neighborhood bordering Rock Creek Park, but to find somewhere we could afford to buy, we had to move either in or out of the city. Sunday afternoons we explored inner city neighborhoods and lost-in-time suburbs, weighing safety and convenience with neighborhood ambiance, visiting open houses and learning what was important to us. In the process, we learned we weren't fixer-upper types. The bungalow advertised as a "handyman special" in Takoma Park, Maryland taught us that. We arrived at the advertised open house but no agents or pamphlets greeted us, only a No Trespassing sign, a front door on half-hinges, and hissing cats climbing in and out of basement windows. Inside the sub-floor was exposed and the house was divided into about eight apartments. A brave soul had whitewashed the whole place except for the dark stairs leading down to the basement and up to the attic. It became instantly clear to me that, as a general rule, I would not go where the whitewash man feared to tread.

Our real estate agent coaxed us to visit a close-in suburb we'd never heard of and we found an attractive Cape Cod bungalow we could move into right away. It was affordable and offered no scarlet wall-to-wall carpeting or residential stray cats. Built in 1929, it had high ceilings, natural wood, and sat on a broad tree-lined street of older Victorian houses. We took the plunge and bought.

Meanwhile, a postcard revealed that Angela and Jack had run aground in Florida due to exhausted funds. "We are torn between staying in Florida where we can find work or pushing on to New Orleans and arriving broke. New Orleans beckons. . . ." she wrote. They knew Louisiana was in an economic depression but were confident they'd find work. Angela got a job in a fast food restaurant and at night they slept in the van, not the America of their dreams but still America. When I heard from her next, they'd limped into Baton Rouge, the capital of Louisiana.

"Jack's found paid training learning to drive tractor-trailers and I stand a better chance here of getting a real job. New Orleans was impossible," she wrote. After months of depending on the kindness of strangers, they were both working and had rented a mobile home on a bayou outside Baton Rouge in Back Brusly, which was pronounced "Brooley." Not Brusly proper, mind you, but Back Brusly. With a roof over their heads and jobs, their outlook was improving. "I was amazed when Jack threw me a surprise birthday party," she wrote, "but what shocked me was when he proposed. We'll go back to England to get married next year on my birthday, September 24."

I hoped my marriage had been an inspiration as those of my friends had been to me. Of course, I couldn't go to the wedding. How tiresome this secretiveness was and how long could it continue? I counseled myself to be patient. Look how much had already been yielded: a mother who wrote to me and sent me books, and a beautiful sister who shared her life in my own country. Angela had invited Jim and me to their homestead at Christmas to experience Back Brusly for ourselves. In her next letter, she announced that Jules, our youngest sister, would be joining us. Her parents were paying for the airplane ticket. "I wonder if anyone's told Jules," said Jim.

I wrote to Eve and made it clear that Jim and I would be with Angela for Christmas. Surely she'd take this opportunity to tell her family. I started to hope. Eve remained silent and as the holidays approached, Angela and I structured a fallback plan. Angela wrote,

---

You'll soon be meeting Jules. Don't worry! Eve hasn't communicated with me, even though she knows you'll both be here at Christmas. If Jules arrives still in the dark, I'll tell her, and she'll have a couple of days to get over the shock before you and Jim arrive.

We agreed it would be better if Jules learned from Eve that she had another older sister. It seemed crazy that Eve wouldn't prepare Jules, but Angela and I knew enough not to expect anything.

Chapter 13

On Christmas Eve, Jim and I sprinted through National Airport to catch a morning flight to New Orleans. We'd dallied at home and almost missed the plane. On board, I took out a pocket compact and checked my make-up. I wondered what Jules would look like as I stared at myself in the mirror. I'd seen photographs of her that showed a resemblance between us. I'd sent Angela a letter of introduction and a photo of myself. I rechecked my hair. This concern with appearances would be superficial for most people, but as an adoptee starved of reflections of people who looked like her, visual similarity was the beginning of a new life. Not a new life exactly but a new sense of oneself as being fully alive and rooted in the world. Part of my mission to Louisiana was to mason my old world with my new.

We didn't know whether Eve had told Jules. Meeting a new sibling under such circumstances has to be on the list of Ten Most Stressful Occasions, yet I wouldn't have exchanged the agony for a winning ticket in a five million dollar lottery. My first family reunion. This was the family I'd broken rules to unearth. My first Christmas with the only blood relative who'd chosen to choose me. I couldn't be much happier. Like the ordinary people seated around me on the plane, Angela and I were gathering with our spouses and boyfriends for the holidays.

Our plane screamed to a halt and taxied slowly to the terminal. The weather was cloudy and warm, and the ground crew worked in shirtsleeves. With a silent prayer of encouragement, I strode up the corridor to the gate trying not to seem eager. No one was there.

"What now?" asked Jim.

"They'll be here," I said, thinking of the times I'd been late picking up Angela at the airport. This wasn't how I'd imagined our meeting.

"Perhaps they're waiting in the terminal," Jim nodded toward the security gate. Of course. People had to wait on the other side of the X-ray station for arrivals. We walked along the wide corridor, taking in the travel posters, scanning the crowd as we approached the barrier. We passed through. No one was there. But a minute later, Angela, Jack, and a scruffy young punk with a shaved head walked toward us. I'd planned my introduction: "Hello, Jules, nice to meet you. This is my husband, Jim."

Instead, I clumsily ducked past Jules, embraced Angela, and escaped to greet Jack. Behind me, Jim introduced himself. Ever self-centered, I'd imagined Jules as a younger version of myself: wavy hair to the shoulders, a skirt, a shy smile. Not this stout little skinhead in a leather jacket with a face like a blank sheet of paper. I was shocked but tried to act natural. I wanted to stare at her but stole glances instead. It hurt to make eye contact. I wanted to ask her what if anything Eve had said, but her sullen face held me at bay.

Jim didn't feel as constrained. He chatted and charmed us through the airport to the baggage area. "How do you like America?" he asked Jules as we waited for our bags.

"It's different," said Jules.

"So, you're sisters!" Jim offered. "This must be awkward; we know lots about you and you don't know diddly-squat about us." We all went to the snack bar for something to drink. Angela and I got coffee while the others found a table.

"Did she know?" I asked.

"No, I had to tell her," mumbled Angela.

"How did she take it?"

"Not too badly," Angela's lukewarm smile betrayed her understatement. We drank our coffee, and I showed them a photo of our new house and where it was on the map. It all felt like a sham except for the glances at Jules. Staring at her straight on seemed rude but I couldn't stop trying. When Jack and Jules walked over to the money exchange counter, Jim said to Angela, "It's rather difficult, isn't it?"

"It'll be fine," Angela said breezily. On their way to the airport, the muffler had fallen off the van, now named *Alien* in honor of their immigrant status. As we left the New Orleans airport, the drizzle turned to heavy rain and the old van leaked in a half dozen places. Consequently, the eighty-mile trip to Baton Rouge was loud and wet. Angela placed me in the passenger seat next to Jack—a queen on her throne—while Jim and Angela hunched on a bench in the back and Jules tried to anchor herself on the floor. I aimed several well-thought-out questions at Jules, but in the din of the muffler-free van, I finally settled down to watch the damp green Louisiana countryside slip by.

As we neared Baton Rouge, we stopped at an auto parts store to buy a new muffler. I hid behind the tall shopping center sign to grasp a moment of privacy. I heard a commotion and when I reappeared, they were all standing in a row, looking for me. I felt like an idiot. "We thought you'd run away," said Angela as we climbed back into the van. I *wished* I'd run away. I offered my dry seat in the front but got no takers. Next we stopped at the Lynnvale Shopping Center for film, and I bought some Carefree chewing gum and offered it around. Everyone took a piece, including Jules. Could we all please be carefree now?

At a pay phone a few miles from home, Jules called her boyfriend. She needed lots of quarters and when she ran short, we contributed what we had. Angela and Jack teased her as she chatted at international rates about the warm weather. Jim and I ambled around the parking lot, taking pictures of the 350-year-old live oak tree and the meeting place bulletin board. A deputy sheriff's car was parked cozily next to a trailer. The store attached to the pay phone was closed for good. Jules wished her boyfriend a merry Christmas, and we climbed into the van for the last leg of the trip.

Angela and Jack were renting a three-bedroom trailer at Morley Marina, a collection of eight trailers in various states of disrepair and a large one-story hangout called Ted's Place. The trailers perched between the riverbank and the bayou, and a large railroad bridge spanned the water just north of the marina. When they opened the trailer, a wave of hot mildew-scented air assaulted us. "Very nice," I said. Although earlier it had been too wet to walk around the French Quarter, by now it was a lovely day for December, warm enough for a T-shirt.

The trailer's stuffiness improved after we opened some windows and turned on the fans. In the center of the living room sat the world's largest color television console with a VCR on top. "It's a rental," Angela said. "We pay almost as much to rent the TV as we do to rent the trailer," she said, "but we love watching movies, so it's worth it." I marveled at her capacity to soldier on despite obvious obstacles. Did Eve have this same capacity to make the best of things? Did I? I wasn't sure when I saw our bedroom. "I hope you like wildlife," Angela said. "Not cockroaches, we got rid of those. Lizards."

Sure enough, the place was full of small brown and green lizards, in the bath, on the windowsills, on the walls. Fortunately, I'd grown up with an amphibian-crazed brother and didn't mind them, except for the one that fell on me while I was lying in bed. Angela and Jack had the master bedroom in the front. The bay window overlooked the river and the parking lot. From there, everyone's comings and goings could be observed. Jules was staying in a small bedroom directly behind the living room. The trailer had two bathrooms; the more functional of the two was off Angela and Jack's room, and the other was next to our room.

Angela's bathroom challenged my sense of decorum. The area around the tub was rusted out because there was no shower curtain. Every surface was waterlogged and a sodden brown bathmat soaked my socks when I walked on it. Jim, the more useful of the two of us, pulled the bathmat outside to dry in the sun.

Arriving home, we sat down for a snack. There was Cajun fried turkey sent over from Ted's Place, bread, cheeses, chips, dip, lettuce and tomato, cookies, cake, and candy. Jules and I laid the food out in a buffet, and we sat down for our first meal together. We were still sneaking looks. That ridiculous British restraint began to smother me again. The British among us insisted on ignoring the obvious, and the Americans were outnumbered. One by one neighbors dropped by to meet us and bring good wishes. Shortee arrived with sheets for our bed. She was a pretty, chatty blond who was Ted's seventh wife and lived with Ted in one of the trailers across the parking lot. She bubbled as she talked and opened and closed her observations with "Hello!" as in, "Hello! I was drunk as a skunk last night and Ted came home and wanted me to help him with them turkeys and I said, Kiss my ass! Hello!" I found her charming.

"Y'all sisters?" she asked. "You don't look nothing alike!" Half-sisters, we assured her. Then Doug, who was courting Annie in the trailer next door, came by to see how we liked the fried turkey. He said it was first marinated then fried. Setting aside our quasi-vegetarian ways for the occasion, we'd found it delicious, with a dark brown skin, savory and crisp. He motioned to my cowboy boots, "I saw them boots as you was gettin' out of the van. . . you like country music?"

"I like all kinds of music," I told him. Later, I poked fun at him and said, "I bet you like both kinds of music, Doug, country and western," but he didn't get the joke and nodded in earnest.

Jules and Angela had decorated a tree and hung fairy lights all around the living room. The tree glinted and winked. I placed our Christmas gifts alongside theirs under the tree. After watching a movie, we walked out to the river. The full moon shone on the water and the earth shimmered. We walked up the road then cut through the woods to the railroad bridge, an impressive steel span with a watch house twenty feet above the track. When the barges came through, the bridge opened by disconnecting and raising the train track and watch house straight up in the air. Jack said he had stood on the bridge while it was raised. "It took me above the top of the trees and left me there for twenty five minutes," he said.

The frogs sang. A fat buzzard perched on the beams supporting the bridge. The watchman's radio muttered river news. The muddy river flowed quickly, carrying logs that looked like alligators. Jack said you could hear a train coming from miles away. The lights of a barge approached in the distance. I walked off the bridge to behind where it disconnected from the main rail. I'd had enough ups and downs for one day without going to tree-top level. The others laughed at me but eventually left the bridge too, and we walked back to the trailer. The clear sky was bright with stars.

Back inside, we sat on separate sofas watching the news. More on the downing of the Pan Am flight from London. We ate the chocolate chip cookies I'd baked. I'd put M&Ms in them as well so they'd be a crowd pleaser. I wanted so much to please the crowd. I wondered if I'd made the right choice in coming. Perhaps I should have retreated when I'd learned Jules would be there. Perhaps what I'd seen as a fortunate confluence would derail all the relationships I was trying to build. For the first time in my search, I wondered if I'd made a mistake.

At bedtime, our room was lit by a floor lamp with a naked bulb. No lizards in sight. A pair of cheap white sandals hung in the closet, remnants of the former occupant, I decided. Not Angela's taste. The sheets were clean and fresh. As I climbed into bed and felt the mass of soft springs give beneath me, full of uncertainty, I whispered to Jim, "I don't think I'm going to make it." It was the soft springs inside me that I doubted.

"Sure you will," said Jim. "Imagine we're camping in the mountains. This is deluxe." There was nothing I could do. I cozied up to Jim. Thank God he was so accepting of my family adventures. I was lucky to have a mate who'd follow me to Back Brusly for a Christmas to remember *avec* lizards. Our bedroom had no door, so I'd opened a utility closet door that covered half the space. We snuggled in, tired. "Good night, Jules," Jim called out to the next room.

"Good night," she said.

"Good night," I said.

We arose on Christmas morning, drank dark Community coffee, and watched the neighbors through the bay window. Ted's daughter was visiting her mother Annie next door. Annie was one of Ted's previous wives. His daughter Caroline was gay and arrived with her girlfriend. The girlfriend carried a baby, rumored to be Ted's child. Such was life on the bayou, better than the soaps.

"Look!" said Angela, holding up an enormous turkey. Jack's firm had given it to them for Thanksgiving and they'd frozen it for Christmas, Thanksgiving not yet meaning much to these new immigrants.

"I love cooking turkey," I said.

"She does," said Jim. "She once cooked a turkey the size of a Volkswagen."

"I'd be happy to help," I offered.

"No," said Angela, "I'll do it. It can't be that hard." I stepped back, not wanting to be pushy.

"Where's that pan I bought?" asked Angela. "Jules, find the package and see how hot the oven's supposed to be." Jules poked around in the trash and studied the shreds of plastic turkey wrapper. "I can't find the instructions," she said.

"450 degrees for 15 minutes, then lower it to 350," I said before stopping myself. Soon I was cooking. But I hadn't been pushy, I hadn't insisted. It came down to who could get it done, who would move into the mother-vacuum. With the turkey in the oven, Angela and I sat in the front bedroom and watched river society wake up to the holiday.

"Have you had time to look at 'my thing?'" Angela asked, referring to the travel journal she'd asked me to read. Angela was a good writer with a distinctive voice. I assured her I'd finish reading it that day. "Don't be nice about it," she warned. "I want to know what you really think. It's probably just garbage." Shades of Eve's lack of confidence.

"Don't criticize your work," I said. "The Muse of Art doesn't like it. The important thing is to keep writing. Write, *celebrate*, let the work go, and write something else." Of course, this was the advice I gave myself. The most challenging aspect of being a writer was letting go of the work, accepting its imperfections, and moving on.

"But it's so hard," she said. I nodded my understanding. Lizards scampered along the windowsill as we sat on the unmade bed in the bright sun, two sisters talking about writing.

At noon, Jules wanted to call her parents to wish them a happy Christmas. It was a stunning day, warm, breezy, and clear. I put on jeans and a T shirt with a red heart pierced by a gold thunderbolt on the left breast. I thought about staying at the trailer and reading but decided to go along. I should have stayed home. We piled into the van to go to the pay phone. I took Angela's manuscript. I wanted to say to Angela or Jules,

"Please say hello from me," but I felt they'd disapprove, that they, like Eve, thought I had no right to make myself known. I felt as if I was a solitary line and they were a part of a circle. This holiday was the intersection of their family and mine. I wanted to be present, yet our point of intersection was hypodermic sharp.

At the pay phone, we tumbled out of the van. Jules tried to make the call but the lines were busy. Jim took more pictures of the live oak. I tried to take a picture of Jules but she turned and squeezed deeper into the phone booth. I pretended to fiddle with the aperture. When Thomas answered and Jules began talking, I raised the imaginary rifle secreted in my heart. The law enforcement officer within said, "Freeze!" I could have guessed I'd feel this way and I came anyway. I lifted the barrel of the gun, and the skinhead in the phone booth bobbed in the cross hairs of my super-scope. The voice inside said, "Drop it," but I fingered the trigger lightly and waited. "Steady," the voice whispered. I was listening to everything they said, hardly breathing.

"Hello, Mummy!" Jules exclaimed. "It's lovely, we're wearing T-shirts!"

With each exchange, I sank into a miasma of self-pity. Images of saying goodbye to my parents and the spartan dormitories of boarding school flooded my mind. I felt like an orphan. Then jealousy smoked in my heart. What had I done to be cast out? I could kill them all for not acknowledging me. At that moment, the skinhead turned in the phone booth to face me and I glimpsed the impish smile of someone I knew very well.

I sighed and put the safety catch back on my interior rifle. Dropping onto a tree stump, I opened Angela's manuscript:

We crawled into New Orleans on our last dollar and desperately looked for work. At night we tried sleeping in our van in the Shoney's parking lot on St. Charles Street, but the August nights baked us like French bread.

As I read, Angela talked to Eve and passed the phone back to Jules, who eventually hung up. "Mum said I should be sure to send her baby home safely," Angela said, teasing Jules. *What the hell,* I thought, and picked up the rifle. *By the time I was Jules' age. . . .*

But I let it drop again from my shoulder. Jules' innocence and dependence on her parents made me burn, but it wasn't her fault. She wasn't even born when I was sent to boarding school at age eight or immigrated to the States at twelve. I recognized my real target was Eve, who hid behind her two daughters, my sisters. And them, I wouldn't harm.

I nursed my sore heart as we rode home and they chattered about who had got what for Christmas and how their family was spending the day. I'd speak to Jim later when it was safe. Jack wanted to say howdy to some people in a trailer on the way, but Angela, ever practical, was concerned for the turkey, which we'd left in the oven. "I'll only be five minutes," he said, but she was wise to the locals.

"It'll be 'Come on in y'all. How d'yall like Back Brusley? Have some turkey, why don'tcha?' Take us home first, please." Jack relented.

My bird was beautiful as usual. I told them my favorite turkey-cooking story about the twenty-nine pound bird I couldn't lift after it got hot, and everyone laughed. The day wasn't a total waste; I'd claimed my ground. I might be a Jane-Come-Lately, but I was a turkey-cooking champion. Amid the aroma of cooling turkey, Jules and I rested at the kitchen table and, for the first time, looked deeply into each other's eyes.

"When I saw you yesterday," she said, "I was shocked. You look exactly like the photos of Mum when she was young. I didn't expect that." *Good,* I thought. *Genes don't lie.*

"I was shocked by you, too," I admitted.

"Did you ever look for your birth father? And why did you look for Eve?" she asked. Later I realized I didn't answer her question squarely. I gave her the sanitized reply. The real answer scared me and would have scared her too. I told the story, not of why—I attributed that to deep-seated curiosity—but of how. The documents and searching, the heart-stopping phone calls, the hot catches and cold trails.

"It's strange that of all the daughters, Nicki should look the most like Mum," said Angela.

Even as I wanted to shoot Eve, I loved hearing that I looked like her. "It's kind of scary," said Jules.

"How was it when Angela told you?" I asked.

"I wasn't surprised," she said. "Nothing Eve does would surprise me." I didn't know enough about Eve to know how true that was. Jules was another window into Eve's life. I peered in, but Jules protectively folded the subject up like a napkin and turned her attention to dinner.

"Will you help me lift the turkey out of the oven?" I asked her.

The flimsy foil roasting pan was full of fat. Working together, we carefully lifted it onto the bread board and off the oven door to the counter. It was gratifying to do something together. I wanted to do things for her, find her a coffee cup, hand her a fork, because when she accepted, I felt accepted. Perhaps it was only a trick with mirrors but that didn't matter. Angela had been thrilled to find me; Jules seemed neutral with subtle flares of hostility. How much of their different reactions was due to Eve's behavior? I suspected a great deal, but it also underscored how different even blood relatives could be. A chillier family circle than the one I'd hoped for came into focus, a family of veritable ostriches. I wondered what role British class snobbery played in Jules' coldness. Perhaps she was snubbing me because I'd been born illegitimate, a sentiment Angela was unlikely to share since she too had been born to a single mum, but most likely it came down to Eve's fear and our makeshift introduction.

To escape from my preoccupations, I carved the turkey. I told Angela I'd had a fantasy of us eating Christmas dinner outside in the sunshine. "What a wonderful idea," she said. Jim and Jack carried the kitchen table and chairs outside. Jules set the table with a special cloth, Christmas napkins, and two kitschy angel candles that melted from the head down. We took pictures of the magnificent table and of us, Jules of me, me of her, us of them, all of the turkey. At least Jules was becoming less shy of the camera. The neighbors were highly amused at the British invasion dining outdoors. Cajun Bob the engineer and his girlfriend came over to wish us a happy Christmas. He managed to wangle from Jim that Jim's Daddy was from New Iberia, Louisiana.

"*Parlez vous Français?*" he asked him, but Jim wouldn't admit to any skill at all. I've noticed men are shy about speaking foreign languages because they're afraid of looking ridiculous. Like many women, I felt ridiculous so much of the time, I couldn't see what difference barbaric French would make, but Jim just grinned, shook his head, and retreated.

Jules remained distant. As soon as we started to make headway, she'd recede like the tide, like Eve. I knew the visit must be stressful; she who only a day ago discovered the particulars of her mother's secret life. The only one in her family who seemed to take me in stride was Angela. Sitting in the sun, she looked around the table and raised her glass. "To family and friends," she toasted optimistically.

After dinner, we went to Ted's Place for a drink. The bar was a low gray barn of a building clinging to the edge of the muddy river. They used to have a phone, Angela said, but there had been trouble and it was taken out. Ted himself was a hard drinking man with a twinkle in his eye. It didn't surprise me he was on his seventh wife; he looked like a man who enjoyed women. He used to drive tractor trailers with Jack but lost his job when he tried organizing a union. "Ted's been kind to us," Angela said, as he bought us all drinks. Jules and Jack played a game of pool while we watched. When they'd finished, Jules came and sat down next to me.

"You just got married, didn't you," said Jules. "Angela showed me the pictures. Your dress was beautiful," she said. I told her about our wedding.

"I wish you could have been there," I said. Then without knowing why, I asked, "Do you like children?"

"Yes," she said, with enthusiasm, "very much. I'd like to be a teacher." Behind her thorniness, I saw that Jules had a gentle, sweet disposition. The baby of the family, she wasn't overly mature for her age, yet she watched out for her own interests. A pushy, toothless man named Old Roy saw me watching him dance with Ted's wife and called out that I was next. When I declined the offer, he nuzzled up to Jules instead. I found my back going up, and Old Roy must have felt the heat because he rapidly moved off to bother someone else. When I turned to Jules, she gave me a cool glance as if to say, "I can take care of myself, thanks."

"Jules has always been very attractive to men and boys, even at a young age," Angela told me later. At nineteen, Jules did nothing to enhance her looks. The sides of her head were shaved with only a little more left on top. She wore no makeup, an old T shirt, black jeans, and stout black shoes. Yet one by one, the men of Back Brusly had eyes for none other. She possessed an appealing grace that seemed genuine.

Back in the trailer, we made coffee and warmed up the Cajun Christmas Cake, a log of cinnamon coffee cake, studded with nuts, raisins, and cherries. Before opening presents, Angela wanted to read us part of her travel journal. She read about how happy they'd been when Jack found work in Baton Rouge. They'd moved into the trailer park in Brusly, and after a string of character-building minimum wage jobs, Angela had landed a waitress job at a tony French restaurant in downtown Baton Rouge. With an English accent and fluent French, she made good money. It was easy to see why she was grateful for her new home, no matter how rustic.

We watched as they opened their family presents. I'd already received a book from Eve and a card from Moira, their grandmother. Angela and Jack got elegant bathrobes from Jules and Marianne. They modeled them for us and looked glamorously out of place in the trailer. Angela opened our present, a striped Mexican blanket in electric blue, her favorite color. Even though she didn't have much money, Angela had bought a music tape for Jim and an art poster for me, "Something for your new house," she wrote on the card. I handed Jules a small package to open. It was a sterling silver ring in the shape of a mask that a jeweler friend had made. She slipped it on and it fit. "Nicki has one like it; so do I," said Angela. Jules seemed to like it.

"Cult of the Mask Ring Women," said Jim.

Jules handed me a card. It was a simple merry Christmas message. "I'm sorry I don't have anything," she said, faltering.

"That's all right," I said. "What would you have given me, a card saying, 'How are you . . . and *who* are you?'"

"It was terrible how I told her," Angela finally admitted. "I was so nervous, I wanted Jack to be there but he was working. We went to Wendy's. We'd ordered our sandwiches and I asked Jules if Eve had said anything before she left. She said no, so I said, 'It's like this: You know my friend Nicki? Well, Eve had another daughter a long time ago. She's your sister.'" My heart sank for poor Jules.

"I wasn't shocked," Jules insisted. We gazed at each other. What would I have thought if someone had broken such news to me at nineteen? "But I couldn't finish my sandwich."

I wished that Angela had found a smoother way to tell Jules. Without Eve's help, Jules had no idea who I was or what I knew; of course she was defensive. She might have thought, "Why trust someone my mother is ashamed of?" All I could do was offer my empathy and respect; I was powerless over the barrier Eve's reticence had erected.

In England, the day after Christmas was Boxing Day, another winter holiday. In Louisiana, it was a gorgeous, spring-like day on the river. By the time we awoke, Jack had left for work. I took my coffee and leftover cake down to the picnic table on the dock and wrote in my notebook. Jules joined me and stretched out on the bench with her eyes closed. Can we ever be friends, I wondered. Her pale eyelids were still. I wrote and said nothing. Before long, some hunters drove up to the slip and backed their boat into the water. It was strange to see hunters set off in boats, but Louisiana is made up of swampy land floating in waterways. The boat sputtered off, encumbered by two men and a boy dressed in camouflage, a set of guns, and several coolers.

Christmas hangovers had caused a boat trip that Angela had arranged to be called off, but Ted's wife introduced Jules and me to a pair of hunters who said they'd be happy to take "some young ladies" out for a spin around the bayou in their motor boat. "Just a moment while I get my camera and the others," I said. Neither Sherman nor Al were glad to see Jim tagging along as a chaperone but we cheerfully piled into their boat, and Jim, giving me one of those "I hope you know what you're doing" looks, climbed in after us. Sherman took immediately to Jules as the only unattached female. Soon she was at the helm and we hurtled along, hair and wind streaming in our faces.

It was impossible not to laugh and feel exhilarated, flying through the bayou with my two sisters; much better than sitting in a musty trailer staring at each other. Although I knew we might never do it again, we were adventuring together, something we daughters of Eve were born to do. A few miles downstream, we docked at a cabin. Everyone who hunted seemed to have a shack they used as a base camp. The woods were dotted with them on both sides of the river. On the bank lay a buck carcass, head and hide only. Jim, the true vegetarian, gave me a look.

"We have to keep the carcasses around for when the game wardens come by. Can't shoot does right now, only five point bucks and up," explained Al. He was quieter than Sherman. He told me he was originally from Alabama, came to Louisiana during the height of the oil boom, and stayed for the hunting. Sherman returned to the boat with his rifle slung over his shoulder, and we motored slowly upriver as the hunters scrutinized the bank for deer tracks. After they found the deer crossing point, Sherman told Jules to turn the boat into the center of the stream and pull back on the throttle. Water streamed gray green behind us as the river disappeared between the banks. A few miles of roaring along and Sherman again slowed the boat, mooring it at a place we could get out and walk. In the woods, there was a creek to our left and the ground looked marshy. We stayed on the trail. "What kind of animals are in the woods?" asked Jules.

"Snakes, possum, 'coon, armadillo. You scared of snakes?" Sherman asked Jules gleefully.

"No," she said and serenely walked on. He tagged along next to her, considerately pointing out trees and signs of animals by putting his head close to hers and touching her shoulder. After walking awhile, we returned to the boat and motored home. Spanish moss and fan palms gave the scenery a tropical look. I watched for crocodiles but all I saw were logs in the swollen river. Back at the dock, Sherman tried to make a date with Jules but she adroitly slipped out of any commitment. "That was an adventure!" I exclaimed to Jim when we were alone. "If you don't mind sitting in a pool of deer blood," he grumbled. "When the guy with the gun saw me get in the boat, let me tell you, I heard 'Dueling Banjoes' playing." Eventually, Jim polished the tale of our river excursion until it became a jewel in his bizarre story collection; for the moment, he was relieved to be on dry land away from firearms.

Angela and Jules planned to drive us to New Orleans so Jim and I could spend our last day in Louisiana exploring the city.

Though Jack had spent much of Christmas Day beneath the van, we weren't sure the repairs on Alien would hold. As we set off, I opened the passenger side window for some air and mysteriously, the whole fixture—glass, frame, and all—was immediately sucked out of the vehicle. We stopped to retrieve the remains, but the old window had vaporized. Then it started raining hard. We stopped at a convenience store and bought duct tape and trash bags and covered the window opening. After fifteen minutes, the new muffler fell off. Boiling mad, Angela pulled into a gas station. "That's it," she said. The mechanic's face clouded over as he walked toward the vehicle. She'd have to leave it, he said. Jim suggested renting a car.

"What a spectacular brother-in-law you are!" said Angela. Within an hour, we were back on the road in a sturdy rental. When we got to New Orleans, we strolled the French Quarter and ate lunch before driving to our hotel in the Garden District. Angela promised to return the car on time the next day. Jules and I wished each other farewell in the parking lot. She assured me she would write, and I told her I'd taken some good shots on the boat and would send her copies of the photos as mementos. She was reserved; I couldn't blame her. It was a strange situation. Outwardly, I was optimistic but deep down I felt discouraged about the impression I'd left. Nothing to do about it; soon, Jim and I were alone.

Chapter 14

If I said I love the sculptures of Donatello, novels of the great Russians, William Faulkner (not so much as formerly) & Bashevis Singer & the Victorians, esp. Dickens. If I said Greece was in my soul, & the Greek language moves me as no other. . . . If I could quote Hopkins & too much Eliot, does this tell you more about me than knowing the colour of my eyes, the shape of my legs, or the arrangement of the room in which I sit?

Eve, May 1989

When she couldn't reach Angela, Eve wrote and asked me to pass on messages. She was grateful that Angela had a friend in America and thanked me for helping her. I helped Angela because she was my sister. I was happy Eve acknowledged that relationship, and who could say how much of what I did was not really to please Eve? She even started writing news of Jules, though I never heard another word from Jules herself.

As Angela and Jack's wedding approached, I felt isolated again. It would be different from my wedding in which everyone who wanted to be was included. When Angela invited her former housemates in Maryland, Eve misunderstood and thought Angela had invited Jim and me instead. She lashed out to Angela: "Burn this letter after you've read it. I can't believe you'd betray me like this! Never mention it again. . . ."

Angela and I commiserated. Eve's outbursts were not reserved just for me. They were always followed by silence and mumbling remorse, but never apology. She seemed to have never learned the simple art of saying, "I'm sorry, I goofed." Though I understood how unbalanced Eve could be, I still wanted to be accepted in her family, which perhaps showed how unbalanced I was. So I prayed, I went to an adoptee-birth-parent support group meeting and talked about Eve, I went to adult children of alcoholics meetings, I wrote angry letters and threw them away, I forgave, I took it back, I forgave again. Accepting Eve was exceedingly hard work.

Angela had bought her dress and was making plans. "Of course I want you there, but it's all down to Eve," she said. That didn't give me any hope. Secretly we were both longing for Eve to have a change of heart, but we knew it wouldn't happen. Angela's dad sent them their airline tickets home from Louisiana before she could ask to be routed through Washington. They went back to England in August 1989 and married in September. Jim and I sent them a set of wind chimes for their house in Louisiana. Angela sent postcards, news, and photographs. Eve sent nothing. By the time Angela and Jack returned in the fall, I was thrilled to have the whole thing over.

After the New Year, Angela told me Eve and Thomas were coming to visit them.

"You're not expecting her to visit, are you?" asked Jim one day at breakfast, after I'd spent a sleepless night. "She's going to disappoint you, she always does."

"I know."

"As long as you know," he warned.

"How can she come to my country and not visit me? It's unfair," I railed.

"You know what a certain president said about unfair." Jim was trying to get me to see the situation as clearly as he did. I felt better being angry than choking down disappointment. I drew nasty pictures of Eve. I tortured her in my imagination then shot her thoroughly with a machine gun. I used a portable tape recorder to record vicious letters. I played them back to hear myself telling her what a rotten, selfish, cowardly human being she was. Then I decided to call her.

"You sure you want to do that?" asked Jim.

"It's all very well to vent into my tape recorder," I said, "but I want her to know how I feel."

"You run the risk of losing her," he said.

"I can't go on like this." Though I was afraid of the consequences of telling the truth, breaking the silence swept me forward with the force of a wild wave. I rehearsed our conversation and burned up as much resentment as I could. I didn't want to dump every unexpressed feeling I'd ever had. I simply wanted to say I was disappointed that she wasn't coming to see me as well.

I was terrified as I dialed; number eleven of life's ten most stressful situations—hadn't I experienced enough? The phone rang. It wasn't too late to hang up. A young woman answered. I asked for Eve. She asked who was calling and I said, "Nicki." It must have been Marianne. My heart pounded like rotating helicopter blades.

Eve came to the phone. "Hello?"

"Is this was a good time to talk?" I asked.

"Yes, fine," she said. She sounded breezy and cheerful. But as soon as she got wind of my frankness, she wouldn't let me get a word in edgewise. "I love you," she said, "but a visit is out of the question. There isn't time, and there's Thomas. Utterly impossible. You must *not* expect so much from me. I *do* love you, I think of you often. And I gave you Angela." I imagined Angela as a rotisserie chicken in some deli. I stuck to my script.

"I know I can't change you," I said, "but I'm disappointed, and I wanted to tell you that."

"I'm glad you rang but I must go. I'll get in touch with you by phone during my visit." She hurriedly hung up the phone.

I wished Angela hadn't told me they were coming. The whole time they were in the States, I sensed her presence and waited for the phone to ring. A letter arrived on New Orleans Marriott stationery, which I opened lightheartedly, expecting "Had a wonderful time in New Orleans. Sorry no time to ring but think of you often. Love, Eve." In other words, a typical Eve-a-gram. Instead, she wrote,

---

Dear Nicki,

Please do not telephone me for emotional chats. It is not the thing. I am a private person & I intend to stay that way. I'm sorry, but I will not be emotionally blackmailed.

No date, no signature. I broke down in tears in the kitchen. Jim ran into the room. "What's wrong?" He read the letter. Eve viewed communicating as "emotional blackmail."

"Don't write to her anymore," said Jim. "She doesn't know how to be decent. Why do you keep trying to make up to her? All she does is disappoint and hurt you." He felt bad because I cried even harder. It was my worst nightmare; no hope, no common ground. I cried all night and almost destroyed her letter, but my writer's instinct told me to salvage it. I longed for revenge but decided to do nothing.

Three weeks later, a card arrived. "You open it," I said to Jim. I'd sworn I'd send her letters home unread, marked "Return to Bloody Sender," but I couldn't do it. I stood in the dining room while Jim read the letter silently in the living room. I didn't even want to be in the same room with her letters.

"It's all right," he said. "She's remorseful and likes you again."

Dear Nicki,

Your restraint is super. Thank you. You are a terrific girl. Book, letter will be sent, appropriate for a playwright. I thank you. I'm treading softly. Be sure I think of you.

Love from Eve

It hadn't occurred to her that I hadn't written because I was devastated. No apology, no "I'm sorry I behaved like a jerk." I was happier being back in her favor, but our relationship had run aground.

The book, *A Theatrical Casebook* by Peter Brook, arrived in June. I didn't read it. I couldn't be bought off with a paperback anymore. The card read,

---

Dear Nicki,

Peter Brook is about the only non-fiction writer I read. He's a strange offbeat one—hope you like him. We're all one-off people (aren't we) like clowns, posturing, grotesque, magic, not to be taken seriously. Have fun this summer with Jim.

Love to you both from Eve X

"One-off? Grotesque?" Speak for yourself, I thought. There was no birthday card in July, only silence. After a few months, I got tired of being angry. I didn't want to react the way she had with a slammed door, but I wouldn't go back to swallowing every humiliation. In the fall, I sent her some snapshots from our vacation in Hawaii. I wrote her news about my writing, my house, my friends. I encapsulated The New Me in a single sentence at the end: "I was hurt by your New Orleans letter." If she couldn't take that, she couldn't take me. No response.

"You've come a long way with Eve this year," said Jim. I was wrapping a Christmas present for Angela.

"Right down in the ditch," I said.

"Look at it this way: you'll climb out, she won't. You're better off. You have me." He hugged me and I felt tears come then dissipate. I saw myself mud-covered, climbing out of a drainage ditch next to a glassy lake.

The next day, I felt peaceful. No matter how she acted, she loved me: I knew this by now. She didn't mean to be hateful; she was afraid and guilt-ridden, even narcissistic. Not unlike me, except that I kept climbing out of the ditch. Her problems had nothing to do with me; it only seemed that way. She wasn't the dream mother I'd wished for. This was an abiding disappointment, but I was learning to accept disappointment graciously. Through the struggle of building a relationship with this exquisitely private person—some would say closed—I'd always detected her love. The first words she ever spoke to me, "I don't want to get involved with your life, but I am curious," turned out to be an accurate blueprint of her intentions. Was it simply curiosity that continued to bind us together? I never wanted to believe the first part of her statement. I'd been sure I could change her, but I couldn't.

The results of my search were clear. It didn't matter if I never received another greeting from her or Philip. I had what I had come for, a sense of who they were and in some part who I was.

That I didn't receive everything I'd hoped for was regrettable;
that they'd both given all they were capable of was apparent.
The next day, a card arrived:

HAPPY CHRISTMAS.

*For Dear Nicki, With love from Eve. Little parcel following
(I inadvertently sent it surface mail). Keep happy, I hope all
goes well with you & Jim. I do thank you so much for your
discretion. I think of you.*

Yes. X

Chapter 15

In the years following Moo's death, I'd considered visiting England but didn't want to risk more rejection from Eve. My contact with Philip trailed off after I got married. I still sent him Hanukkah cards and a photo each year, but he seldom replied, and I didn't pick up the phone to find out why. A psychic reader once told me, "Your relationship with this Philip is not about father and daughter. There are barriers between you, but when the time is right, it won't be hard for them to come down." That made as much sense as Philip's silence. He was warm when I put forth the effort to contact him, but he never wrote or visited on his own initiative.

Jim and I decided to spend a couple of weeks in England visiting my family and seeing Cornwall in the southwest, ending the trip with a few days in Amsterdam. I wanted to present the best possible face of my native land so we went in June, hoping for good weather. I wrote to Philip and Eve to let them know I was coming in case they were interested in seeing us. Angela was already in England, she and Jack having returned for a few months to recall why it was they'd left in the first place.

"Eve would like to have lunch and meet Jim," Angela wrote encouragingly. The only day convenient for Eve was the day we arrived, but as long as Eve realized she'd be getting us jet-lagged and scruffy, I told Angela, we had a date. I heard nothing from Philip; he seemed to have severed ties, perhaps weary of my rebutting his earlier invitations. Then a letter came, sent surface instead of airmail; it had taken six weeks to arrive.

Dear Nicki,

I received your letter and photograph last week. I'm sorry that I haven't written before. You may not believe this, but I have meant to put pen to paper for a year.

Of course, we'd be delighted to see you when you come. Averill and I would like you to stay with us when you come to Nottingham. Louis is now fifteen and Rebecca is thirteen, all growing up.

I've been rather preoccupied with a few problems of my own. My daughter Rochelle is now married with a three-year-old boy—my grandson. I haven't really told you a lot, but I really find writing difficult. I look forward to seeing you both and hearing from you.

Love, Philip

It was hard for me to understand someone not being able to write a letter, but it was wonderful to be invited to meet his family and to be finally willing to do so.

"I've had a few health problems since I last talked to you," he said when I phoned to make arrangements, "two heart attacks, and a stroke last year."

I was immediately contrite. I'd considered only my struggles, forgetting that others might be experiencing their own. We arranged to travel by train to Nottingham and stay overnight with them. Philip sounded relieved that we anticipated a short stay, although twenty-four hours is a long visit when you're entertaining strangers, even intimate strangers as we were.

Four days after I received Eve's luncheon invitation, Angela called with bad news. A lump in Eve's breast had been diagnosed as cancer, and she was going into the hospital right away for a mastectomy. Eve would be home recuperating by the time we arrived in London, but her illness would make a visit "complicated." We met Angela for lunch at the jaunty pizzeria where she and Jack had met, not far from Eve's house in Hampstead. She looked windswept and dashing in a new leather jacket.

"Eve's doing much better," said Angela as she closed the menu with a knowing slap, "but I doubt she'll be in the mood to see you. She's just started venturing out of the house."

But why not see me, I thought. I'm only here every half dozen years. "Please give her my love," I said, passing a wrapped bundle of books I'd brought for her. If only she'd let me do some of the things a concerned friend would do instead of keeping me at a distance. I felt resentful, which I hid from Angela because it was tactless under the circumstances. I asked about Jules.

"I told her you were coming," said Angela, "but I think she's busy at the moment." I'd sent Jules the Louisiana photos but never heard from her. "I guess I'm not everyone's cup of tea," I said, a bit gloomy.

"You are *mine*—and Moira's," Angela said. Moira was Angela's beloved grandmother and Thomas's stepmother. *She* had invited us all for dinner at her apartment. After lunch, we staggered to our hotel, hoping for a nap. The hotel overlooked a beautiful private garden. Our room was supposed to be "garden view" but was undergoing renovations, and we ended up in the back. "River view," the desk clerk said sardonically. In our tiny, freshly painted accommodations at the top rear of the house we found a flower arrangement on the bedside table with a card attached.

Dearest Nicki and Jim,

Welcome to England! I'm so looking forward to seeing you. What fun we shall have!

Love, Moira

Moira Jameson's London apartment, down the street from BBC Studios, had balconies on three sides filled with potted geraniums and azaleas; "my garden," Moira called them. Elegant in a straight black skirt and cream silk blouse, she met us at the door. "Darling Nicki, I can't believe I'm finally meeting you!" she said and swept us into the apartment. "I feel as if I've known you for years, don't you? Jim, what a dear you are. Angela has told me all about you. She absolutely dotes on both of you. Let me take your coats. Oh, what fabulous flowers—my absolute favorite. You are too sweet."

From someone else, Moira's effusive style might seem false, but she was sincere. She opened a bottle of champagne to celebrate and we settled into the soft cushions to wait for Angela. The telephone rang and Moira spoke for a few minutes before I realized that the caller was Eve. Moira was patient and solicitous; Eve was obviously confiding in Moira about her recovery. Jim and I chatted awkwardly.

"That was your dear mother, of course," said Moira as she hung up, not one to beat about the bush. "It must be annoying to have to sneak around. But what can we do? I'm glad you're here with me tonight. Can I top up your glass?" Angela arrived straight from her job at a real estate agency and was worn out. Moira, with unbridled fondness, fussed over her and gave her a glass of champagne. After Angela was settled, Moira disappeared to put the finishing touches on dinner.

Moira served us homemade cream of spinach soup, chilled scotch salmon and baby garden vegetables, with fresh strawberries and cream for dessert. We whiled away the hours as the London lights twinkled below us. When Angela, who had to work the next day, left in her car, Moira came downstairs to help us hail a cab. Before we could stop her, she pressed a twenty-pound note in the cabby's hand, saying, "Please drive them to their hotel and take good care of my darlings. They're precious to me." After we told the cabby our destination, only a short distance away, he said, "She must think an awful lot of you, that's all I can say. Grandkids, are you?"

"Something like that," said Jim.

The rest of my time in London I dodged the rain and tried not to think of Eve. This was the second time I had visited England and she'd refused to see me. She neither called nor sent a message by way of Angela. On our last night in London, we were moved to a dank, cramped room on the first floor of the hotel. "Can't sleep?" Jim asked, as I rolled over for the twentieth time. My stomach burned.

"She didn't even call."

He put his arm around me. "She doesn't know what she's missing," he said.

"It's not meant to be, is it?" I asked him. We snuggled in the damp darkness; a truck rumbled by outside. "I'm finished waiting for her," I said.

"I know," said Jim.

"Tomorrow we can leave London and see Philip."

"Just one thing," said Jim, "Don't let me order Guinness this time, all right?"

Chapter 16

We left from old St. Pancras, the Central London station that services the British Midlands. Its swooping iron and glass train shed, erected in 1868 during the reign of Queen Victoria, boasted the greatest single-span roof built up to that time and dwarfed the trains attending the platforms. As we entered the station, we passed through an enormous red brick gothic structure, the former Midland Grand Hotel, once the classiest station hotel in the capital, now demoted to municipal offices.

Lacking the lively bustle of Euston and Paddington, which served the wealthier western and southern counties, St. Pancras waited patiently for its northbound customers, who passed in ones and twos beneath the mammoth station clock.

"It's lovely to leave the city," I wrote as we passed English pastures filled with flowering yellow mustard and grazing sheep. "Leaving commerce behind. Here comes the Old England, albeit graffiti-covered; red brick buildings, graceful spires, and day hikers."

Philip was on the platform when we pulled in an hour later. We got off at Loughborough, a town closer to his house than Nottingham center. We were still in the country, a respite from the grimy gloom of the city that had yielded nothing but superficial pleasures and disappointment, I thought bitterly.

To my relief, Philip looked just the same as he did five years ago, only slightly grayer. No disfigurement from the stroke, which had been minor. Actually, he looked happier and more relaxed than at our furtive meeting in the bar of the Nottingham hotel. Of all the faces, his was the most familiar. The depths of his soul I knew little of, but his face I grew up with and loved. He greeted me with a touch of humility. It was as if my presence stirred something unexpected inside him. His son, my brother Louis, was waiting near the car, where Philip introduced us.

"You like Run DMC?" Jim asked, as the sound of rap pulsed through the open car window.

"Yeah," said Louis, "and LL Cool J."

"He just played Washington," said Jim.

"Did you see him?" Louis asked eagerly.

Jim laughed. "Afraid not. But I try to keep up."

"He was playing Birmingham but my Dad wouldn't take me," said Louis, carefully stepping on Philip's foot.

"Imagine that," said Philip, opening the car door. "Wouldn't drive my son four hours to a rock concert. Terrible father, I am."

"Dad! It's *rap*, not rock!"

I sat behind Philip and could see his face in the rear view mirror. Every once in a while, he looked at me and smiled.

"We'll stop for a drink at the local, shall we?" he said. The Sunday afternoon sun shone on the bucolic countryside. I liked his lilting Midlands accent, a question at the end of each sentence. It wasn't a fancy accent like Eve's; more like steaming porridge on a cold morning or homemade gravy at Sunday lunch. It was the old-fashioned accent Moo used when she'd slip her arm through mine as we strolled the gypsy markets looking at hamsters, handbags, and shoes, "What larks, Pip old chap, what larks!" Like his face, the sound of Philip's voice was a comforting place to come home to.

At Philip's local pub, we ordered drinks. I kept mine a juice, wanting all the sobriety I could muster. Louis ordered a vodka and orange to Philip's amusement. He was only fifteen. In Europe, it's not uncommon for teenagers to occasionally drink with their parents at the pub. Philip bet Louis he would be carded, but he wasn't, to Louis' satisfaction.

"I think I look at least eighteen," he announced to us.

"What do you think?" Philip asked us.

"Yes," I said, "eighteen, maybe twenty."

"Really?" asked Louis.

"Maybe forty," said Philip. "What do you think, Jim, fifty?"

"I dunno," Jim said. "Ever since I turned sixty, I can't see without my bifocals."

"He's not. . . he's joking, right?" said Louis, unsure whether Jim was a miracle of science or pulling his leg.

"Very good for sixty, I think," said Philip.

"Dad!"

I liked Louis, tall, fairer than Philip or me, easygoing, friendly. Philip was an affectionate father, bantering back and forth with him. We drove home, a spacious farmhouse surrounded by fields, with stables in the back. As we arrived, Averill, Philip's wife, and Rebecca were hitching the horse trailer to their car to go to Rebecca's riding lesson.

My sister Rebecca was thirteen and olive-skinned like me. She said hello and averted her eyes when we were introduced. I didn't know what she knew. What would I have thought if my father had brought home a 35 year-old woman when I was thirteen and said, "This is your sister"?

After we unloaded our bags, we tried to find the riding school to go watch the lesson. We drove back and forth along country lanes, Philip and Louis muttering to each other.

"It was down there, Dad."

"No, it wasn't. That's the other place, the one with the jumping paddock."

"I thought that was down there."

"No, that's the other place they go to."

"I hope you don't think we're always this disorganized," Philip said to us in the back seat.

"We're enjoying the ride," said Jim.

We found the field at the end of a country track. A cold wind had picked up and we pulled on our jackets. Several students were taking a cross-country jumping class. Philip introduced us to friends who were watching the lesson. Rebecca rode her powerful dun gelding with authority. When she trotted over to us, we patted the horse. The whole family enjoyed horses. Since I'd been the only rider in my family growing up, it was pleasing to have this passion in common.

Lesson over, the horse was loaded into the trailer for the drive home. Sitting at their long wooden kitchen table, we drank tea. British reserve prevented us from being too direct. Instead, we talked around the subject. As soon as we leave here, I thought, I'll need a vacation.

Louis was the more outgoing of the two kids and brought to the table family photo albums of trips to Israel, Disney World, and France. I discovered Philip had been to the States a couple of times in the past few years. Why had he never called?

Rebecca's way of saying hello was more obtuse. They had two dogs, a German shepherd and a terrier. First she brought the terrier up into her lap, making a fuss of it, introducing him to me. Then she called over the shepherd, and I introduced myself. In her reticent manner, she was saying, "We like animals, do you?" As Averill made dinner and I flipped through albums with Philip and Louis, one by one, Rebecca brought to the table the cat, the rabbit, and the guinea pig.

"If it's stopped drizzling outside, perhaps we could go meet the horses?" I asked. I didn't want her bringing them to the table. The suggestion was met with enthusiasm, and we followed Rebecca and Louis out to the muddy pasture to meet four Fell ponies and several horses. I fussed and nuzzled the ponies; Jim made his acquaintance from behind the fence.

Averill made a wonderful dinner of *coq au vin*, vegetables, and three different desserts. "I didn't mean to make three," she said. "I forgot all about the trifle. Never mind, we can all get fat," she said. We drank red wine, and Louis told Averill about his vodka and orange in the pub.

"I shouldn't have thought you'd like the taste," she said.

"It was rather good," he said.

"Next, he'll be tending bar for us," she observed calmly.

After dinner, we helped clean up and watched TV in their television room, which was tucked between the kitchen and the dining room. It was filled with dozens of family photographs, hanging in frames and leaning against each other. I was pleased to see some of mine, our wedding photo and a recent portrait. The pictures fascinated me: There were my grandparents, Philip as a boy and as a young man, his other daughter Rochelle, Rochelle's son, Miles, and Philip's younger brother, my uncle Jeffrey. I yearned to request copies of some of them but didn't feel comfortable asking.

We relaxed on the sofa and watched Averill's favorite Sunday night shows, a couple of comedies and a variety show that was an unusual mix of silly English comedy and investigative journalism, sort of "Laugh-In Meets 60 Minutes." The terrier settled in my lap. I loved relaxing with the family, doing what they'd do on a Sunday night.

Around ten o'clock, Louis and Rebecca got ready for bed, and we watched the news. Philip talked about his business and how he'd coped with the recession.

"What would you like to do tomorrow?" he asked me.

I'd already thought of this: "I don't know if it's possible, but I'd love to go horseback riding."

"That's the easiest thing in the world," said Averill.

"I didn't bring any gear," I said.

"You look about the same size as Rebecca. I'm sure we can outfit you," she said.

"Right then," said Philip, smiling. "We'll go riding."

The spare room where we were sleeping was downstairs next to the dining room. After everyone else had gone to bed, I padded back into the television room to gaze at the gallery of family pictures, especially the one of Philip taken when he was about four years old. He wore a black beret and looked so like me, it could have been my own childhood portrait.

I arranged the photograph under the light of my bedside lamp and took a picture of it. I didn't know if it would come out, but it might. The house had an alarm system and while I was moving around, I heard strange beeps and bleeps, so I returned to our room. Jim was asleep in a single bed by the window. My mattress felt soft as I pulled the covers over me. I turned out the light and as I drifted off, I thought, "I'm falling asleep in my father's house. . . asleep in my father's house."

I rose early to say goodbye to Louis and Rebecca before they went to school, then went back to bed. Averill was a homemaker and Philip was semi-retired. The four of us breakfasted together. "That was my second breakfast," said Averill.

"I had to give up everything I liked when I had my second heart attack," said Philip. "It's funny how you get used to things. I never thought I'd be able to eat skim milk on my cereal but it doesn't bother me at all now."

"I'm glad I don't have to eat it," said Averill. "I like a bit of fat with my food. But you," she said, leaning over Philip's shoulder to kiss him tenderly on the cheek, "are very, very good."

"The doctor told her to be encouraging," Philip added, winking.

I liked them together. Philip's wit was dry and Averill was every step his match. They seemed to genuinely enjoy each other, and Philip appeared grateful for the rich domestic world Averill had created.

Averill gave me a pair of Rebecca's jodhpurs, a jacket, and a selection of boots and socks. Rebecca and I were exactly the same size except her feet were bigger. Stuffed with socks, her short boots fit me fine. Jim declined to ride.

"No," he said, "never touch the stuff. I'll walk instead."

"If you go out of the gate and down the road twenty yards, you'll find a public footpath. I'm sure the dogs would be pleased to show you, it's their favorite walk," suggested Philip.

"Good," said Jim, "while you ride, the dogs shall take me for a walk."

I was given a Fell pony to ride, a solid, dark-haired lady who'd won many awards. I was sure she'd take good care of me. I hadn't ridden in a couple of years, but it was like riding a bicycle, you don't forget. In fact, my muscles would remember all too well, but that wouldn't be till tomorrow. Five of us rode: Philip, on Rebecca's handsome mount; Averill, on one of the young boarder horses; and two of her friends, also riding boarders. Jim did gate duty and took pictures. Soon we were clopping down the road, staying on the shoulders where we could, parading through the classic Midlands countryside.

The area where Philip lived was still dotted with stone cottages, tiny churches, and old farms surrounded by low stone walls. This was the Old England again, before McDonald's, motorways, and MTV had made it seem more like the 51st State than the heart of the United Kingdom. Philip pointed out where a farm recently had been subdivided for houses and talked about his neighbors, gesturing left and right. There was little traffic on the road and that which came by gave way to us. After riding for half an hour, Averill and her friends turned back. The young horses had had enough and the riders had work to do. It was, after all, Monday morning, and not everyone was on vacation.

"Would you like to continue?" Philip asked, swiveling in his saddle.

"Yes," I said. My rear end was sore but this was an opportunity to seize. The others turned back and we rode on, doing a circuit on the country lanes that would bring us back to the house. It began to rain lightly. Philip was dressed in jodhpurs and an ancient oilskin mackintosh. He looked like a dark cowboy in the Wild West. Once we were alone, he questioned me.

"Will you be seeing Eve?"

"Depends on her," I said.

"It's terrible to admit," he said, "but I don't remember what she looks like."

I didn't like the idea that my father couldn't remember what my mother looked like although it was perfectly logical. He hadn't seen her—even a photo—in thirty years.

"She looks like me," I said, "but blonde. A bit ravaged but charming in her way. I've only seen her once myself," I added, "but I do have pictures. Angela sends me pictures and Eve did once as well."

We were strangers, the three of us, barely remembering what the other looked like; thrown together in a moment of biology, simmered as genetic soup, bound by my persistence to get to the bottom of a mystery. And this was the bottom. They would never have sought me out, or each other. I was the link, a lightly magnetic force between two carved images—a man and a woman—my birth parents and my most intimate acquaintances. I pondered them like Easter Island statues. I circled and touched them, when they let me, trying to interpret the meaning of their detached gazes out to sea.

Philip and I reminisced about our small shared past, how shocked he was to hear from me, how his memory returned regarding the circumstances of my birth.

"Did Eve say she saw me after you were born?" he asked.

"No," I said, surprised. "Do you think she did?" I imagined Eve shadowing Philip.

""I just wondered," he said. "It was. . . it was a long time ago."

We cantered for a stretch, leaving me breathless. "What kind of Jewish family did you grow up in?" I asked, as we walked, stirrup to stirrup. "I was told it was conservative and that's why you didn't marry Eve. Is that right?" The moment to ask questions might never come again.

He looked puzzled as if wondering why I would want to know something so arcane. "Yes," he said, "I mean, my mother and grandmother kept kosher, if you know what that means."

"I do," I said. "I have lots of Jewish friends."

"We went to temple, not all the time but regularly. You'd say we were Conservative. Now it's different." Averill wore a gold Star of David necklace. She must have converted. There was a Star of David on the lace tablecloth in their dining room too.

"Now we're what you'd call Reform," he continued. "I try to get the children involved. Louis is taking Hebrew classes and Rebecca goes to various temple activities."

"And you celebrate the Holidays?" I asked.

"Yes," he said.

"I'm exploring Judaism," I told him. "It's not an easy religion to worm your way into, but I've always felt Jewish and I'm drawn to it in spite of what people say."

"What people say" was the dilemma of having a Jewish father and a non-Jewish mother. Every time someone innocently pointed out that I wasn't really Jewish, I wanted to query a rabbi: should the transgressions of Jewish fathers be borne entirely by their outcast half-breed children? What of the men who, like my father, abandoned their non-Jewish lovers and children? Do the Scriptures not require them to atone in some way?

I didn't share these thoughts with Philip, but I wanted to talk about it. He was my Jewish family. I wanted to know what it meant to him and tell him what it meant to me. This might be our only chance.

"When I was growing up," I ventured, "one of the only things I knew for certain about myself was that I was Jewish. The trouble was I didn't know what it meant. I didn't even know it was a contemporary religion like Church of England or Catholicism. I thought it was something simply historical. I never met another Jew until I went to the States when I was twelve years old. Yet I knew I was one, that it made me different, in looks and in personality. I had someone's face. I had your olive skin. I even went through a period when I thought I was really a gypsy. Neither of my parents knew anything about Judaism. The mystery made it even more important to me," I told him.

Philip was a decent person. I sensed he felt guilty about what he'd done as a young man. Abandoning Eve, his silence and neglect, then his forgetting. He'd urged me to build a bond with him but had made few moves himself. Guilt held him back, perhaps. I didn't want to add to it.

We rode on quietly. The narrative of mystery ran through my mind like a litany: When I'd told school friends I was a gypsy, it was because gypsies were the only English people I saw who looked like me. When I did well in school, my mother said it was because Jews were clever. When I was sneaky, my aunt said it was because Jews were sly. I was in the 10th grade before someone explained that observant Jews followed particular dietary rules and didn't eat pork.

When we moved to the States, I made my first Jewish friend, Lisa Gottlieb. She and her divorced mother were brassy and full of life; I loved visiting their home. At Christmas, we sang a

Hanukkah song along with Christmas carols for the high school choral concert. When I talked to other Jews, they invariably asked which of my parents was Jewish. It hadn't mattered in England where there didn't seem to be any other Jews at all, but in the States, my Jewish identity was probed and dismissed. I learned to be defensive when I saw the question coming. People didn't realize how much it hurt to be told that I didn't belong to the Tribe. Why should it matter which side the genes came from as long as they were there? I was happy to learn that Reform Jews were inclusive, welcoming people like Averill and me into the fold. I might remain forever on the periphery of Judaism, but I'd always be a Jew, and I wanted an opportunity to explore the faith if I chose to.

I didn't tell Philip any of this. He'd felt no responsibility, walking away from Eve to marry a Jewish woman his parents approved of. He had been twenty-three with the youth and sex of a person able to walk away from an unexpected pregnancy. Riding behind him, I watched his body lurch from side to side with the long strides of his horse. He'd told me all he could, and the rest was for me to work out. Though acknowledgement made it easier, I realized I'd never needed his permission to be a Jew, any more than I needed his approval to identify myself as his daughter. I am who I am, I thought, because of them, in spite of them, regardless of them.

I pulled up alongside of him. He looked glum. I sensed his unease with our conversation, as if I were reaching for more than he naturally wanted to give. I changed the subject and told him how happy Jim and I were together. Isn't that what fathers want to hear from their daughters, that they've made a good match and are well taken care of? It was true.

"Do you want children?" he asked.

"Yes," I told him.

"Perhaps I'll have another grandchild by your next visit," he said merrily, and I smiled.

He was grateful for the reprieve from our discussion of spiritual matters. Jew or Gentile, most English people are squeamish when talking about religion, believing a frontal discussion to be in poor taste, like talking about bodily functions or diseases. They'd rather talk about boating, horses, or the weather. With all matters settled, Philip stirred his mount into a rousing canter along the margin of the road, he leading, me following, jumping drainage ditches and skirting unsuspected holes. Half a mile later, breathless, we rounded the corner and found ourselves back where we started at the house. We'd talked as intimately as time and circumstance allowed, and most importantly, I'd held my own completely in this horse-loving family by not falling off.

Chapter 17

Eve was never far from my mind. Obviously, she wouldn't see me. As a result, I looked forward to ending our vacation in Amsterdam. My stay with Philip had been good but twenty-four hours were enough. At the station saying goodbye, he and Averill had wished us well and asked us to come again soon. We all parted satisfied we'd done our best under awkward circumstances. At the airport, I called Angela.

"I'm sorry I haven't had much time for you. It's been madness, between this ridiculous job and taking care of Mum. I hope you understand," she said.

"I do," I said. "Do you think you'll be coming back to the States?"

"We'll be back in the fall," she said. "I'd felt homesick, but now that I'm back, I see it's hopeless here, no good jobs and finding an affordable flat is impossible, and. . . well, England's not for me."

This was good news. For our separate reasons, the cloudy London hustle-bustle was no fun for either Angela or me. Once Jim and I arrived in Amsterdam, the air suddenly became warmer and the clouds lifted. Young people appeared. We walked ourselves silly going to museums, the Anne Frank house, and Indonesian restaurants.

I enjoyed paintings by Dutch masters I knew Eve would fancy. I knew her taste by now. She loved the dark, luminous Europeans. She adored young boys and sensual, lounging women. She reveled in ancient civilizations and remained bemused by the modern. She would have enjoyed the faces of the milkmaids and the stout Dutch burghers, the elegant facades of the narrow mansions along the canals, the hoisting hooks, tidy churches, pealing bells, and ghosts of medieval prosperity and chaos. How wonderful it would have been to walk these winding alleys arm in arm with her, taking in the riotous flower boxes and languishing in cafes over dark coffee and stacks of books. What fun we could have had if we could have had it. What fights we would have had if we had shared our innermost visions; how different we were in the end and how similar.

I whispered goodbye to Europe and hello to home. Home was firmly Washington, D.C., one of the most beautiful cities I'd ever been to. It was my husband and friends, the home of my university and the seat of the government. I'd fantasized showing Eve our museums and galleries, our spectacular vistas and gardens, my country; but as the plane rolled in bumps and jerks toward the terminal, I accepted that that would probably never happen.

To me, Eve was almost unknowable. She didn't know me because she'd locked both of us away in boxes. I remained the dark-haired doll who appeared to her but no one else as a total stranger, whose loss she mourned every day, every year in gifts to friends' children and solitary visits to holy sanctuaries. Thirty years later, I was still not an adult to her, yet I wasn't even the child. I had become only the loss.

To me, she remained the young woman who did the hard work of living the consequences of love, abandoned by her handsome sometime boyfriend. In the startling loneliness of the occasion, a part of her had been killed, the carefree art student, the free-wheeling, free-spirited risk taker, and another woman had appeared in her place. The new woman had the same carefree appearance but inside she bore the old grief like a permanent scar. This part of her, the person I saw, was not the mother so much as the grief. I hated being someone else's loss. It was easy to believe that her loss had something to do with who I was. It didn't, but it always felt as if it did.

I'd created my own boxes, of course. She was also the ever beautiful, perfect mother who, upon my opening the lid, would embrace me with fair-skinned arms and marvel and coo at her perfect creation. She would have no gray hair and make no mistakes. Even the mistake of relinquishing me would not have been her responsibility, but an accident of fate. She was a mother-under-glass, perfect in every way.

Out of our boxes in my imagination, we strolled European streets in mother-daughter harmony, which included dramatic fights and reunions. In yet another box was me, the waif-like *abandonata*, searching, always searching, a victim of circumstance, a perfect stranger, forever foreign even to herself. In the end, my boxes were as confining as Eve's.

Yet Eve's loss was part of what made Angela and me true sisters. We'd both been babies when the choices were made, mere possibilities, not formed personalities. Of the two babies, I had been the one who was lost, and Angela had been Eve's redemption. Eve took the opportunity and blessed it.

"Every evening," Angela told me, "when Mum tucked me in for the night, she always tucked in and kissed my Raggedy Ann doll, the one we'd named Pippa."

We all knew that if not for me, Angela might have been given up. And if not for Angela, I might not have the slim relationship with my mother that I did. Every day, I tried to release Eve from the prison of my mind and prayed to be released. For years, all we'd had was what we'd created in our imaginations. To stop believing the fantasies felt like betrayal. Reality was a tough adjustment.

The boxes were on the shelf now. I wouldn't throw them away even if I could, any more than I'd throw away an old diary. They were once-upon-a-time mementos, like the photo of a first puppy, the memory of a first kiss, and the feel of a first baby's shoe. At Christmas time, Eve surprised me by sending a beautiful golden chain, with a typical note: "I wouldn't deign to choose an amulet to hang on it for you." In the new year, I discovered I was pregnant. I wondered how she'd react to the news of her first grandchild, with rejection or an embrace?

I wrote, carefully omitting the pedestrian word "grandmother." No reply. When Eve and her husband visited Angela and Jack on the West Coast where they'd settled, she made no effort to contact me. I cursed her once again for flying over my country but there was nothing I could do but snarl to myself. That was how she was.

Eventually Angela called me. "Why haven't I heard from you?" she asked.

"I didn't want to bump into Her Majesty, so I stayed clear," I said.

"She didn't stay with me, you know," said Angela.

"Oh?" I said.

"I hardly saw them. She didn't really come to see me. I mean, she did, but it was just an excuse to travel again. She and Thomas went all over, Los Angeles, the Southwest. She's feeling better. She was shaken by the earthquakes though. There were earthquakes everywhere they went."

"Serves her right for coming to the States at all," I said, petulant as a three-year-old.

"Absolutely," agreed Angela, and we turned our discussion to other topics of interest.

It was enlightening to realize that although being the unacknowledged daughter of Eve Langston Wright Saddler was tiresome, being among the acknowledged was no picnic either. Sometimes I confused Angela with Eve, and this visit reminded me not to. Angela, for her human imperfections, was my good friend. Eve was a mystery to us both.

Why couldn't I let Eve go? The truth was we *were* letting each other go, in untidy fits and starts, as quickly as we could, to the limits of our abilities. I loved her, I loved the woman in the boxes, I loved the mystery, and, truly, I had loved the search.

A therapist once told me that ambivalent attachments were the hardest to let go of. Neither Eve nor I was willing to completely let go or be accepting of the other. Our mutual ambivalence might connect us like salt and pepper for the rest of our lives or one day, one of us might sever the tie altogether. If at times Eve's behavior seemed unacceptable, I knew I chose to continue the relationship.

After my son Miles was born in October 1992, I received a letter from Averill. Philip had died of a heart attack while on business in the Caribbean. I was stunned by the news. Telling people was confounding. My father was dead, no, not my real father. My birth father. Yes, we were close. No, we'd only met three times. Yes, I loved him. No, not the same way I loved Daddy. It was different but still love.

I gave up talking about it and wrote poems while the baby slept. I thought about when we'd stayed with them. How I'd slept in my father's house, under his roof and protection, how we'd cantered together along the lanes of Derbyshire. We couldn't do that again. How mysterious life was: a door opens, and one day—while you're occupied with a basket of laundry or a bill or captivated by the milky white pout of a blissful baby—it glides quietly shut. How grateful I was for the time Philip and I spent together. How sorry I was for the loss of what might have been. The letter from Averill rustled as I folded and replaced it in the blue envelope embossed with an "M."

Though he didn't meet his grandson, I was consoled that Philip had seen a photo of Miles, destined for the wall of the TV room. Having unraveled the mystery of the past, the future beckoned and belonged to me, not my birth mother or father. In finding Eve, Philip, and Angela, I'd found what I needed to belong. Although secrets still remained, I was no longer a secret to myself. And that was the end of the story.

Or so I thought.

Chapter 18

I had no contact with Eve for several years. After Angela's daughter, Delphine, was born, I'd watched Eve treat her two grandchildren so differently, it left me reeling. I'd finally mailed her a dramatic goodbye letter:

September 17, 1994

Dear Eve,

The time has come for me to get on with life. When you do a U.S. fly-over, most recently to help Angela when she had her baby, I'm racked by the most unbearable feelings as you choose her and ignore me again. In me and my son Miles, you have the most wonderful daughter and grandson you could ever dream of.

Over the ten years of our relationship, I've learned that your failure to acknowledge me is your business, not mine. Yet be-

cause I am your daughter, I've kept alive the hope that one day you'd embrace me. It's time for that hope to die. You're not the person I dreamed of, and the person you are I can't live with. I'm tired of crying and being rejected. I know you don't intend to hurt me, that you're doing the best you can. That's why it's best for us to stop communicating altogether. I wish you well. I treasure your many gifts, and especially, I thank you for my sister Angela. I thank you for the hour we once spent together, which is all you ever really owed me.

She never replied.

In November 1997, when Miles was five years old, Angela left an urgent message on my answering machine late one night. I happened to be awake, puttering around the house. "Call me right away. We need to talk as soon as possible," she said. She'd left her home number, her work number, her pager. I dialed, prepared for the worst: the return of Eve's breast cancer? A car accident? Angela answered on the second ring.

"I just spoke to Mum. I've something important to tell you," she said. I breathed a sigh of relief; at least she wasn't dead. "She's told Dad about you." My jaw dropped open and wouldn't close again, just like the expression.

"All's well, she said to tell you," said Angela. "She said she'll be in touch."

My mouth was still open. "How did it happen?" I managed to ask.

"An old friend of Mum's, someone she's known for years, came to visit recently. Mum said she was so impressed by how free her friend was, how she could talk about *anything*. I think she decided she no longer wanted to carry the secret. She didn't give me a blow-by-blow but she kept saying, 'Your father is such a wonderful man.'"

Angela and I talked into the night and she related a story about Eve. When Angela had gone to England the previous month, I'd asked her to buy Miles an English children's book about the character *Noddy*. "The *Noddy* books were hard to find," she said, "but at the end of my trip when I was out shopping with Mum, I found two and bought them. Eve said, 'Who are you buying those for? They're too advanced for Delphine.' I said, 'They're not for me,' and left it like that. But Eve persisted, 'Who are they for?' I finally told her, 'They're for Nicki.' 'Oh,' Eve had said. When we went to the cash desk, she said, 'I'll get those' and paid for them. I didn't tell you before but now I can."

By the time I got off the phone, it was too late to call anyone and Jim was asleep. I had a job interview the next morning; it was important to rest. I drank some warm milk and went to bed. All night, I kept waking up with a crazy party going on in my head. "She told him! She told him! No more secrets!" It was like the day I'd first found Philip.

I'd hated sending the goodbye letter to Eve but it marked a turning point. I wouldn't have tolerated Eve's behavior in a friend. I stopped questioning Angela when she mentioned news of home, but I listened attentively. When Angela and Delphine had flown in for my 40th birthday, I'd told Angela about the letter and our separation and we hadn't spoken about it again. Over the next few years, I felt uneasy over the way I'd sent Eve packing. I'd become grateful that my last words to Moo in an Easter card had been expressions of love. Selfish though it seemed, when Eve died, I didn't want to feel guilty of having spoken too harshly. After much thought, I broke my self-imposed embargo and sent her a simple card: "Dear Eve, Happy Mother's Day, Love, Nicki." I didn't expect a reply and I didn't get one.

A year later, I decided to visit England.

"Are you going to see Mum?" asked Angela, "because I have a suggestion. Send her a postcard in an envelope for privacy. Say, 'I'm coming to England with Miles from this date to that date. Would you like to have coffee? If so, let me know where and when.'"

I mailed a postcard in October 1997. The next week, I took a meditative walk around the community baseball field at lunchtime. I was getting excited about our December trip, just Miles and me. Jim had said his Christmas present would be staying home with the cat and the goldfish. "I'll go to England every other visit," he'd said, which was fine.

As I walked the perimeter of the empty ball field, I imagined meeting Eve in a park. "There's Eve," I'd say to Miles. "Run up to her, say hello and run back as fast as you can!" In my mind's eye, I watched my five-year-old sprint to his grandmother sitting on a park bench, and I thought, "If it ever happens, fine. If it doesn't, we'll see so many wonderful people, we won't have time to grieve." I strolled past the tennis courts and the playground, the leaves rustling beneath my shoes, and felt at last a sense of peace. Two days later, Angela rang to tell me the good news.

Perhaps the possibility of meeting her grandson was irresistible. Perhaps my backing off had given Eve the desire to unburden herself for her own good. Or perhaps, a hand of grace had reached down and touched us both. I'd prayed for her to change, then prayed for the strength to accept her the way she was, prayed because it was the only action I had left to employ. In the very week, perhaps on the very day, even at the very moment that I had found peace on the path near the ball field, she had stepped out of the shadows toward me.

We met Eve at the National Gallery in London on New Year's Day in 1998. London was crowded with tourists and shoppers. Miles and I had joyfully lurched down Oxford Street on the top floor of a red double-decker bus and we were disgorged across from the Gallery. Inside we watched Eve daintily descend the steps of the entranceway, a diminutive force dressed in blue jeans and a baseball cap. We kissed hello as if we'd last seen each other yesterday, not fifteen years ago.

"Are you hungry?" she asked Miles.

"As hungry as a lion," he replied, and we went into the cafe where she bought us tea and snacks. I'd brought her a Christmas gift, a calendar by women painters, which she liked.

She too had gifts for us: a disposable camera for Miles and some elegant fragrance and lotion for me from Floris, the London perfumery. Have you seen this movie, have you seen that one, she asked. "How can you possibly survive as a playwright without seeing these movies?"

"I don't get out much," I said, pointing at Miles.

"But they're all on video," she retorted. I dutifully wrote the titles down on a napkin, on which Miles later blew his nose.

"I can't stay long," she said, "I have an appointment. May I show you my favorite rooms here? I come all the time. It's usually as quiet as a church." We walked through the rooms packed with people, coats, and cameras, and she pointed out the Spaniards and the Flemish masters she loved. She noticed the Star of David necklace I was wearing. I told her I'd joined a synagogue.

"What will you do with boy-child?" she asked. I told her he'd started Hebrew school and loved it.

"I'm Jewish," said Miles on cue.

"I see," said Eve. "How wonderful, such a rich religion. Of course," she said, turning to me, "you're only *really* Jewish if your mother is Jewish, which of course yours isn't," she reminded me. I ignored the jab; I knew what I was.

"What are you working on now?" I asked, referring to her art.

"I've given up that amateur stuff."

"Why?"

"Because you should get yourself a proper art education and become a professional."

"You went to art college," I pointed out. I could relax; I was no longer trying to please anyone.

"But I didn't finish my course," she countered. I was privately aggrieved for her but just nodded.

We went to the gift shop to buy postcards and she bought Miles a badge to pin on his hat. When we parted in the vestibule, she gave Miles and me warm hugs.

"I shall be seeing you in August, I imagine," I said. Angela, now divorced from Jack, was engaged to be married to a wonderful Californian named Mike. Jim and I had already planned to go to the wedding and make it a family holiday.

"Yes," she said, "I'm going to have to buy a really, really over-the-top expensive hat for this occasion."

Miles and I had a second family date that afternoon. I'd always wanted to meet Philip's other daughter, Rochelle. She was the daughter of the woman Philip married shortly after Eve announced she was pregnant. We arranged to meet Averill and Averill's gentleman friend, Les, at Rochelle's London apartment for tea. Afterwards, Averill would drive us back to Nottingham for a visit.

Rochelle lived in Chelsea, a classy London neighborhood near the Thames River Embankment. She greeted us, and I introduced my son Miles, 5, to her son Miles, almost 11. The boys disappeared immediately into big Miles' bedroom to play with toys and a drum set. Her apartment had a gorgeous view of Physic Garden and the River Thames.

"You're lucky you didn't grow up with Philip," Rochelle announced after we'd settled ourselves with cups of tea on the sofa.

Averill laughed. "Don't scare her, darling."

"It's true. Philip was fine until you were three or four and had a mind of your own then forget it." This was a side of Philip I'd not heard of before and I was amused. Blond, feisty, with sensuous bee-stung lips, Rochelle's appearance reminded me of my Miles.

"I think Nicki looks like Auntie Rosie, don't you, Averill?" said Rochelle.

"I do believe you're right," said Averill.

"Do you have the Minson vagueness?" asked Rochelle.

"I have great difficulty keeping track of my keys if that's what you mean."

Rochelle and Averill roared as if I'd cracked the funniest joke in the world. "We're all like that," said Rochelle, "it's terrible."

"Even those of us who married in," said Averill.

"I think it's catching," said Les. Averill told Rochelle that Les had lost the keys to his truck the previous week and it took him four days to find them. When I told Jim about the "Minson Vagueness," it entered our family's lexicon in a big way, only my Miles added a surreal spin by changing the pronunciation to "the Minson Vegas."

After tea, we drove to Nottingham. It was snowing by the time we got there and on both nights of our visit, the house lost electrical power. Hung with photos of Philip and family, the old farmhouse was eerie under the cast of oil lamps and candles. But the lounge had a big fireplace, the Arga stove in the kitchen kept the downstairs warm, and Miles and I cuddled up in our big bed in the guestroom while the wind howled in the eaves.

"Let's go see Daddy on the way in to Nottingham," said Averill. My sister Becca, now a friendly young woman of 21, came with us. When we got to the cemetery, we slid on patches of ice and picked our way through mud. I took a photo of Miles standing next to his grandfather's grave. In the Jewish custom, Averill placed some stones, which she'd brought back from a recent trip to South Africa, on the headstone. "I enjoyed collecting these," said Averill. "Philip always liked stones. He was always picking them up and admiring them and leaving them on the dresser."

The storm had blown open the gate to the Orthodox part of the cemetery, which was usually locked, and we slipped in to visit the graves of my grandparents, Anne Mossef Minson and Louis Minson. I photographed their gravesites too. I wanted to remember every name and date. I touched the headstones and traced my people's names with my fingers. I had wanted to be restored to them and now I was. In the cold, wet ground, we dug for pebbles and placed them on the headstones of Anne and Louis.

"Would you like to see the video of my Bat Mitzvah?" Becca asked that evening during one of the brief periods the electricity was on. She fast-forwarded through the tape, slowing down to show Miles footage of Philip and identifying aunts, uncles, cousins, and family friends. "Look, there's Auntie Rosie," said Averill. "Would you like to go see her? She's in a home now. She's 95, but we can go tomorrow before you catch your train." Auntie Rosie was one of my grandmother's sisters, the four Mossef girls from Warsaw. There was nothing I wanted more.

On our way to see Auntie Rosie, we visited Moo's gravesite. The cemetery had changed in the thirteen years since Moo had died. Up and down the rows we hunted until Averill found her. We placed a sand art jar next to her headstone and once again I photographed my young son grinning in the snow.

We parked in the lot next to the Miriam Kalowich House. Averill said, "Here's how we should handle Auntie Rosie. If we walk in and she knows me right away, we'll tell her all about you. But if she doesn't recognize me, we'll just say you're a relative visiting from America." When we walked into the lounge where Rose Appel was sitting in an armchair, she exclaimed, "Averill! How nice to see you. You haven't visited me in months!" and Averill gave me the thumbs-up sign.

"Who's this?" she asked, chucking Miles under the chin. Her eyes were rheumy but darted between my face and Miles'. "This is Nicki, Auntie Rosie. Philip's oldest daughter. She lives in America but she's staying with us and wanted to come visit you. And this is her son Miles."

"Philip had another daughter a long time ago," I explained, taking her hand. "I didn't grow up with him but we became friends. I wanted to meet you."

"And this is Miles?" asked Auntie Rosie, a veil of confusion across her face.

"This is Nicki's son Miles, not Rochelle's Miles," said Averill. "It's confusing, isn't it? They both have sons named Miles!"

"Not Rochelle. . . ." said Auntie Rosie. "I haven't met you before, have I?" she asked, taking in my face.

"No, we haven't met before."

"But I'm happy you came to see me. Tell me about yourself. Have you seen Rebecca and Louis?"Averill had brought some family photos for Auntie Rosie to identify. Auntie Rosie scrutinized them and talked about each person, and Averill annotated the backs of them. She took some pictures of us together. When the prints were developed, our resemblance was obvious, a pair of bookends, the old and the new.

Each layer of searching yielded more questions and more branches on the family tree. Many families have a memory-keeper, someone who remembers names and dates and recites the family stories. Moo was that person in our family while I was growing up and I'd inherited her love of stories. I never tired of sorting through relationships and rearranging the juxtapositions of circumstance.

Before leaving England, I rang Jules, Eve's youngest daughter. "Aren't you thrilled Mum's told Dad?" she asked me. I said thrilled wasn't the half of it. "I'm sorry for not being in touch with you since Louisiana," she said.

"You were put in an awkward position."

"I hated the idea of lying to Dad."

"That's changed now."

She let out a sigh, "Yes. I can't wait to meet Miles at the wedding. We're going to have so much fun."

In August, Jim, Miles, and I flew to California to attend Angela's wedding. Jules was already there and called us at our hotel. "Mum would like to get the business of meeting Thomas out of the way before the wedding. Why don't you come and find us on the beach at Capitola this afternoon?"

We drove to Capitola, a seaside village on the north curve of the Monterey Bay near Aptos where we were staying. We walked along the beach, scrutinizing sunbathers and brave swimmers. I heard a soft voice and turned to see Jules gliding across the beach. We embraced and behind her stalked Eve looking shy but moving forward.

"Long time no see," she said nervously and kissed me on the cheek.

"Only since January," I said, and she corrected herself as Thomas strode up from nowhere. They must have been waiting at the beachside bar. After all the years and fear, Thomas shook my hand firmly and introduced himself.

"I must know what you think of your President's troubles," said Eve, referring to the Monica Lewinsky affair.

"I'll tell you what I think," ventured Thomas. "It's not about bonking. It's about fibbing." I liked him immediately. After a while, Thomas and Eve took their leave. "Please join us for dinner at Zelda's tonight," he said. "Angela and Delphine are coming too. I've booked a table for 7:00."

Dinner was well underway when, halfway through, Jules took Miles and three-year-old Delphine out for a break to play on the beach. Shortly after they returned, Delphine disappeared and Angela panicked in the crowded restaurant. Sharp words ensued among the Saddlers and Jules walked out in a huff. We found Delphine struggling quietly with her sandals in the bathroom and dinner continued. Jules returned and patched things up. The beauty of it was that none of the disturbance had anything to do with us. As Jim remarked when Thomas apologized for the outburst, "Everyone comes from a family."

Angela had booked a room at our hotel for herself and Delphine the night before the wedding and arrived in the afternoon. She was soon followed by Jules and Marianne, Eve's other daughter, the sister I'd never met. I reflected on how much harder it would have been to meet Thomas and Marianne in London while balancing a cup of tea and a cookie on my knee and rhapsodizing about wet weather. Instead, when Eve and Thomas joined us, our poolside party was in full swing, and Eve's four daughters were together for the first time in our lives. As the children hurled themselves in and out of the water, the adults drank, munched, and talked; a happier extended family on a wedding's eve could not have been found.

The wedding was held on the cliffs above Monterey Bay. Marianne wore elegant blue-gray silk with a periwinkle wrap around her shoulders. I wasn't surprised to learn she hated being photographed; she was much prettier and more graceful in person than in the photos I'd seen. Jules was serene in mint, and I wore a long gown of muted yellows and a wide-brimmed hat. Eve was a tiny spitfire in orange silk and white tennis shoes while Thomas struck a debonair note in a timeless blue and white seersucker suit. Marianne's husband accused Jim, wearing a dark suit and sunglasses, of impersonating a CIA agent. Amid the banks of nasturtiums and tall, sad eucalyptus trees, the coastal mist rolled in and out as the minister intoned his welcome.

Angela and three-year-old Delphine were radiant in matching ivory lace dresses. They both carried little bouquets. "She's gone totally over the top!" sputtered Eve as Angela walked up the aisle on Thomas's arm, but Jules hushed her. The splendid coast, excited guests, and sweet stringed music provided an atmospheric backdrop for the ceremony. "We weren't invited to her first wedding," whispered Jim, "but look at us now. Kismet." How surprising to be without rancor over the passage of years. I'd learned happiness happens in its own good time.

Eve was indefatigably gracious at the reception, making a point of talking to everyone. I looked up and she was having her picture taken with a California biker dude wearing a denim vest and a red bandana. I tipped my straw hat to her and she smiled. "This is John, Mike's uncle," she said, her arm snugly around his waist. "We share the same birthday."

Delphine stayed with us on the wedding night. The next morning, Jim drove us to Eve's so Delphine and I could attend Mass with her. Delphine had been baptized in the Catholic Church and Eve was pleased I brought her along. The Capitola Catholic Church was triangular and modern, with three stained glass windows and a great wooden roof. Eve blessed us with water from the font as we entered, and we found seats in a row at the back of the crowded church. Delphine quietly crayoned while we listened to a missionary speak of her school in Brazil.

We all went down for the blessing; Eve took the sacrament and I was simply blessed by the priest: "May the Lord Bless you and keep you and may you live a long and happy life." As we'd waited in line for the blessing, I put my hands on Eve's thin shoulders and felt my eyes welling with tears—I was attending Mass with my mother. She turned to look at me, smiled her crooked smile and rolled her eyes, as if to say, "What a sentimentalist!"

At the post-wedding barbecue organized by Mike's mother, the children played in a paddling pool and we ate and drank some more under the shade of live oaks and eucalyptus. Miles and Delphine hunted lizards under the watchful eye of Mike's brother-in-law.

I found myself next to Marianne at the dining room table. "It was funny when Eve told me," she said. "We'd gone out for the day. We were having lunch at an Asian place where you sit at long communal tables. Eve was across from me and there were people sitting on both sides of us. Eve began, "Do you know about Nicki?"

"I thought she was getting confused with a new movie. You know how she sees every movie that comes out. I said "You mean Jackie Something?" and she said "No, I had a baby in the 1950s." I said, "You mean I have a brother? Cool!" But she said, "Absolutely not, I only have girls." The people eating on both sides of us were leaning in listening, dumbfounded."

The Saddlers were staying on in Capitola, but Jim and I had rented a cabin in Big Sur to regroup from the thrills of the Royal Wedding. We walked on the rocky magnificence of Pfeiffer Beach and watched a Felliniesque parade of strangers frolic in the mist below the steep sandy cliffs. We skimmed fat flat stones on the Big Sur River, hiked down a fire road, through a rock tunnel, and emerged in a smugglers cove of roaring surf and undulating kelp beds. The night before they departed I called Eve from a roadside pay phone. We agreed that we were "well met at Aptos."

On our last night before flying home, we stayed at Angela and Mike's house. She'd hung the photograph we gave them as a wedding present in the dining room. All over their house hung a profusion of paintings, photos, etchings, and posters. A narrow, brightly-colored painting in the living room caught my eye. A young child in a blue smock stood stoutly behind a push-cart, toys all around her.

"That's good," I said. The brushstrokes were broad and defiant.

"Mum did it," said Angela. "That's me." Then she pointed to a doll in the painting and said, "I still have my dolly" and led me into her bedroom. On a shelf near her bed lolled a Raggedy Ann doll. "Not in bad shape considering how much she's been loved," said Angela, taking up the worn doll in her arms. She had blond hair and a pink dress with a "P" stitched on her sleeve.

"Mum made her. She used to make all our dolls and dresses. I slept with her every night growing up. And every night Mum kissed us both." I marveled at the strong current that had drawn

Angela and me together. She placed the doll in my arms and I smoothed the woolly hair. The dolly in the painting with the "P" on her arm stood protectively over Angela's shoulder. "P" stood for Pippa.

Chapter 19

A t age 19, I poached—there's no other word for my unscrupulousness—the Jewish lover of a housemate. Henry was a lawyer sixteen years my senior originally from the lower east side of New York City. He'd grown up in Stuyvesant Town, which along with Peter Cooper Village, provided spacious, decent accommodations for thousands of middle-class New York families beginning in the late 1940s. Henry's father was a dentist and his mother a housewife; his sister had provided his parents with their first grandchild, albeit 1960s-style, *sans* husband. His younger brother was married to a California heiress with whom he enjoyed "the fast life."

Henry and I fell in love and I soon moved into his Washington, D.C. row-house, where we set up housekeeping. His mother's preference would have been that her oldest son *marry* a Jewish woman, but living with a sort-of Jewish woman was acceptable, and his family embraced me. We visited them on secular and Jewish holidays and I was exposed for the first time to Jewish culture from the inside: bagels and delis and boisterous dinner conversations about Israel and city scandals. We also visited the rambling summer boardinghouse Henry's mother and aunt kept in Sharon Springs, New York, north of Albany, where families of Hasidic Jews escaped the city heat from the Fourth of July to Labor Day. What I knew of Judaism could fit in a thimble but, volunteering to grate potatoes into the big white enamel bowl for a dish of kugel, I soaked up the sisters' kitchen stories and furtively stared at the wig-wearing Hasidic ladies knitting in their rocking chairs and chattering in Yiddish on the shady front porch.

Henry wasn't religious but he was well-read and knowledgeable about Jewish history. We attended Passover Seders at friends' houses and many of our friends were mixed Jewish and non-Jewish couples. After Henry and I broke up, I continued to have Jewish friends, drawn magnetically to what seemed like a mystical realm.

When I began dating Jim, he too had many Jewish friends and we were invited to more offbeat Seders. When we married, we included Jewish elements in the service: the mutual prayer of forgiveness before the ceremony and the wrapped glass shattered underfoot at its conclusion. I even called my bachelorette party, held at a friend's hot tub, my "mikvah" or ritual bath. A seeker by nature, I was looking for a spiritual connection and a way into Judaism. Though I'd reunited with Philip, the thousands of miles between us made connecting on the basis of spirituality or religion difficult, but I kept looking.

Two relationships with Jewish women helped me. The first was with Gail, a therapist whose counsel I sought for many years as I tried to make sense of my chaotic family life. A secular Jew, Gail gently probed my idealized notions of Judaism while respecting my desire to learn more. Linda, the daughter of Holocaust survivors and an Al-Anon friend, was the first "spiritual" Jewish person I'd ever befriended. We shared many cups of coffee and conversations about her family and her spiritual path. Linda was engaged to a cantor and it was through them that Jim and I received tickets to our first High Holiday service at a Washington synagogue. It was the solemn Kol Nidre evening service that begins Yom Kippur, the Jewish Day of Atonement. As I looked over my shoulder at the throng of a thousand Jews wrapped in prayer shawls and synagogue finery, my heart soared. I recalled the loneliness of being the only Jew growing up; who knew there were so many Jews in the world? When we rose to our feet and the choir began singing, I was choked with emotion; for all my life I'd heard these melodies in my head. I had returned home.

Ten years later, standing on the bimah, the platform at the front of a synagogue in Greenbelt, Maryland, I gazed out on a hundred and fifty faces. The Rabbi held the yad, a hand-shaped pointer used to follow the words of the scripture in the Torah scroll. As he pointed to the Hebrew letters, I sang out my verses: *Key-e-e shay shetyamin, asah Adonai. . . "*

The verses I sang were the Fourth and Fifth commandments from Exodus, the story of the journey of the Jewish people. This adventure in Torah reading had not been anticipated by any of us. Eve and Philip had viewed my interest in Judaism with bemusement, but finding them and seeing my ancestors' faces in our family albums had emboldened me. When Miles was born, the question naturally arose about spiritual education. Would my husband and I do something or nothing? If something, what would it be? The answer was clear for me and Jim was supportive. For his first few years, Miles the toddler was my cover as we attended children's High Holiday celebrations and enrolled in Torah for Tots classes. Little did the teachers know who the real tot was.

We eventually found Mishkan Torah, a friendly Reconstructionist-Conservative synagogue not far from home. Before Miles started kindergarten, I worked up the nerve to talk to the Rabbi about our formally joining the congregation. Since I hadn't been raised Jewish, I had to make sure we'd be welcome, but I needn't have worried. Rabbi Griffe encouraged me to join and study, and that was how I wound up in his Adult B'Nai Mitzvah and Study Group. Starting in January, fifteen mostly middle-aged women and a few men met every other Wednesday. It seemed as if every night we had study group it poured with rain, but wet weather didn't dampen our spirits. As we prepared for Judaism's "coming of age" ceremony, we ate cookies, talked, and read the *Book of Ruth* and *Pirkei Avot,* a collection of rabbinic wisdom.

The Rabbi made cassette tapes for us to practice with, one of our individual Torah and Haftorah verses, and one of the complete Festival service we would help lead on the day of our *B'Nai Mitzvah.* I'd learned that it's a *Bat Mitzvah* ceremony for a girl or woman, *Bar Mitzvah* for a boy or man, and *B'Nai Mitzvah* in the plural. During class we learned many such definitions of Hebrew and Yiddish terms and discussed everything from the best ways to give charity to the symbolism of hairstyles.

Many of the others were as nervous as I was to begin with. "I won't be able to attend all our sessions," said one. "I can't read Hebrew," announced several others. "We'll learn what we can," answered the Rabbi. "When we're finished, we'll know more than we knew before, and that's the essence of study." With his gentle prodding and generous sense of humor, by the end we were all singing Hebrew and donning our prayer shawls like pros.

Two weeks before we were "called to the Torah," Rabbi Griffe asked to speak to me. "Which parent of yours did you say was Jewish?" he asked. My heart lurched as I replied, "My father." I didn't like what the Rabbi suggested, that I go through a formal "conversion" procedure before I participate in the *B'Nai Mitzvah.* That I go before a council of three rabbis, a *Bet*

Din, who would question me on my knowledge and faith and validate my "conversion." That I complete the process with a ritual bath, a *Mikvah,* recite the blessings, and emerge Jewish.

"You don't need to do this for Jewish Reconstructionists," he said, "but for other Jews. . . well, I'd hate for you to come this far and have trouble later." I felt my anger rise. Why should I have to prove I'm Jewish? I thought. What difference did it make if it was my mother or father who was Jewish when I didn't grow up with either of them? However, he was right that I hadn't come this far to call it quits. I agreed, and the Rabbi made the arrangements. "We don't have to call it Conversion," he said, kindly. "For you, it's a Reaffirmation." I took a morning off work and arranged to meet a friend at a huge synagogue in the city. Rabbi Griffe and two other rabbis asked some simple questions that I answered honestly; I bathed, said the *Shehekianu* blessing, and returned to work in the afternoon. I didn't like having to perform these rituals to be judged properly Jewish. I was a Reconstructionist; I didn't believe that Jewishness was passed only through the mother's lineage. God the Father got an earful from me on various topics for the next week or two, but in the end, He and I decided to bury the hatchet.

On a glorious Sunday at the end of May, the synagogue was decorated with flowers for the Festival of Shavuot. Shavuot, the Jewish wheat harvest, also marks the commemoration of the giving of the Ten Commandments on Mt. Sinai. Up on the *bimah* with the Rabbi, we joined in the opening prayers. We read Torah and Haftorah, some straight from the Hebrew and some from transliteration, English renditions of the Hebrew sounds. We also made statements on our personal experiences in the group, Israel's 50th anniversary, the *Book of Ruth,* and the scripture readings.

The Rabbi entreated us to continue studying, words that were bittersweet because we'd learned he'd soon be leaving the congregation for a new position. As *B'Nai Mitzvah* gifts, he gave us each a copy of *The Wanderings,* Chaim Potok's history of the Jews. Following the service, the entire congregation enjoyed a luncheon that we'd prepared as an impromptu *B'Nai Mitzvah* project.

I didn't know the words to all the prayers. I sang those I knew and hummed along to those I didn't, secure in the knowledge that no matter what, I surely knew more than I'd known five months before and a universe more than I'd known five years before. At lunch, the Rabbi said, "It finally hit me. Do you know what your Torah portion was? The Fifth Commandment!"

Though the verses had been randomly assigned, the coincidence hadn't escaped me either:

Honor thy father and thy mother,
That thy days may be long upon the land
Which the Lord thy God giveth thee.

Eve had been cancer-free for ten years since the original diagnosis of breast cancer, but eventually it returned. Over several years, the cancer spread painfully to her spine and became untreatable, and in the autumn of 2000, Eve died. She and I had wrested three satisfying years together, with visits to her home, family dinners with my sisters and their friends, movies, plays, and gallery shows. A few days before she died, we talked on the phone about God and death. I sat on the wooden swing on my front porch in blessed November sunshine. When she asked me about faith, I told her I believed that we don't have to be Mother Teresa to receive comfort and strength; a little faith can go a long way.

"Giving you up was the worst thing I ever did in my life," she admitted. "I never forgot you. I'm so happy you found me."

My heart grieved for her years of suffering and I thanked her. "I had a good childhood," I said, and I meant it. "I know what you did was hard. I never, ever blamed you. You did what you thought was best. I just knew that one day, we would find each other, and I'm so glad we did." She died before I was able to visit again, with Angela at her bedside. We all attended her funeral.

The next summer, Eve's husband Thomas rented a large cottage in Aldeburgh. This was the seaside town in Suffolk where he had first met Eve, a single mum with her toddler. Eve and Angela were living in a tiny stone house amid the fishermen, artists, and summer folk. After Eve and Thomas married, they'd kept her stone house as a weekend getaway. Angela had spent all her summers there growing up and had grown to love Aldeburgh.

Jim, Miles, and I flew to London and were driven out of the city in a car Thomas had arranged. Angela, Delphine, and Jules were already in Aldeburgh when we pulled up to the house. It was a joyful reunion. For eight days, we swam the frigid seas, ate local crab, picked fresh strawberries, and endlessly walked the sunny promenade. Almost every shop—the bookstore, the candy shop, the jewelers—held stories of Eve that my family related to me. Here were the inspirations for Eve's pen and ink drawings: fishing boats, stone cottages, and higgledy-piggledy rooftops and stairs. Angela even introduced me to Joan and Betty, two lifelong friends who cycled the promenade every day and served as the town's mobile gazette. *"Ooh,"* they gushed, *"she doon't 'alf look like our Eve, doon't she?"*

Many an evening we idled in the back yard with its splendid purple and pink fuchsias and painted gypsy caravan, painting sea stones with Auntie Jules and playing soccer. Among his throng of lively daughters and friends, Thomas graciously included us, setting three more places at the family table and pouring two more gin and tonics before dinner. We were fully expected to hold our own and contribute to the plentiful talk of literature, politics, and art, but that part was easy.

The Aldeburgh beach is miles of slippery gray shale, pebbles, and rock interspersed with nuggets of gleaming cornelian, citrine, and amber. The great gray North Sea rolls majestically in from the east.

"She swam almost every morning," said Angela.

At midsummer in England, the sky begins to lighten at four o'clock in the morning. Well before five, I shook Angela's shoulder gently and placed a cup of coffee at her bedside. She buried her head of thick blond hair beneath the pillow. She had asked me to wake her at sun up.

"It's all right," I whispered, "go back to sleep." Angela was not a morning person.

"I'm coming," she growled from beneath the covers. "Don't you dare go without me."

Wrapped in towels and fleece, we trudged into a gleaming morning of blue sky and pale light. The breeze kissed us curiously. The gulls wheeled, swirling like white-suited acrobats. At water's edge, an elderly woman rose dripping from the sea.

"How's the water?" I asked, knowing the bone-numbing truth.

"*Lovely!*" the lady replied as she wrapped herself in a white terrycloth robe and glided back to the promenade.

Toes in, Angela shrieked.

"You don't have to get in," I repeated. "Just wait here for me."

"Bloody hell, I'm getting in," she said. "You first."

Navigating a foothold on the steep shale was tricky as the surf pushed and dragged me. A deep breath, an airborne pause, and I crashed through the surface of the sea, emerging seal-like, honking and crying out.

It was the coldest water I'd ever swum in; colder than Brighton in December, colder than the Thames on a raw March afternoon, colder than any outdoor swimming pool at the start of summer, far colder than the Atlantic beaches of Delaware or Cape Cod.

"It's freezing!" cried Angela.

"Swim!" I yelled.

We swam fast straight out to sea, swam for survival, swam to keep from turning to stone. I heard Angela kicking in my wake. We swam full out for several minutes then paused; our limbs had become accustomed to the cold or gone numb or both. The sun rose before us, a carpet of glittering golden stars dancing on the water's surface. Gold all around us. Golden water reflected in my sister's eyes. Like heavenly mermaids, we reached toward the golden stars and swam all the way up the sun.

Afterword

"If only. . . . I wish. . . . "

When we talked before this book was released, Angela had begun, "If only. . . Eve came across better in your book. Philip comes off pretty well. I wish. . . . She was a truly devoted mother to us. I wish there was a way to show this, to show how *she* suffered. . . ."

The California coastal mountains stretched from north to south behind Angela's house. Evening fog began rolling in from the north as we spoke, filling the mouth of the valley with smoky undulation. I explained that a memoir is a deeply-felt story from *one* person's perspective. I'd told everything I knew of Eve's heart. She'd refused to talk about the past and kept me sufficiently at a distance that I could only guess how she'd really felt.

"She didn't want to be found, you know," said Angela, "in the first few years after you'd met. This is probably hard for you to hear but that's what she told me." The reality of publicly revealing the story was causing tension between us. For all she'd shared with me, how many conversations with Eve had Angela kept to herself?

"I know," I said. "When I first met Eve, she'd told me matter-of-factly that as soon as she'd received my letter of introduction, she'd gone to the bathroom and vomited." Not an auspicious beginning. "She was always ambivalent toward me. One day I'd get a come-hither card and a book; the next week she'd push me away with a warning not to intrude, over and over."

"I know it's your book but I wish Eve. . . ." I pushed my feet deeper into borrowed slippers and wrapped a blanket around my shoulders. The evening chill came swiftly to the valley. "She was devoted to us, especially when we were smaller. She handmade our dolls and sewed our clothes. She cooked wonderful meals and took care of the house and all of us."

"I believe you," I said. "I can see by how you mother Delphine and create such a welcoming home, she must have been a wonderful mother—to you. But that wasn't *my* experience of her. This book isn't a novel; I can't climb into her mind and create reams of narrative about her innermost feelings that she never shared."

"I know. Eve was afraid of Thomas finding out. She didn't want to do anything to hurt him," said Angela. "He'd already taken a risk marrying her and adopting me. His family called Eve 'that gypsy' when he'd first introduced her, did I ever tell you that? They were extremely cold to her but he'd held his ground: this was the woman he intended to marry."

"He must have been brave," I said. "He was a good husband and a good father to you. He's a good man." I said I didn't believe that Eve ever wanted to hurt me. "I could be wrong, but I don't believe I ever harbored ill will toward her when I was growing up." As soon as I'd spoken, I felt the faint metallic taste of an untruth. I'd *deeply* resented my mother leaving me and remembered, as preverbal memory, howling with fury at being abandoned. How dare she leave me! At the age of four, when I became aware of my circumstances, I'd determined with singular focus that I would find Eve when I grew up. To punish her? To pull the curtain on her elaborate puppet show? I don't believe as a small child I was that calculating. No, she and Philip had bred me with a potent homing instinct to which I succumbed, with all the fractured feelings and untidiness it entailed, but without malice.

"When you write your book," I said to Angela, "you'll tell a different story. And then the shoe will be on the other foot."

"If only. . . . I wish. . . ." are the engines of stories. I wrote this book to share the story of my adoption reunion, but *each* adoption story is unique. I love these stories and may publish more books about the adoption experience.

I'd be delighted to hear from you, my readers, for future books.

Nicole J. Burton
P.O. Box 54
Riverdale Park, MD 20738
U.S.A.
Website: NicoleJBurton.com
E-mail: Nicole@NicoleJBurton.com

Resources

A memoir is not a how-to book. With the advent of the Web, searching is different and much easier. Nevertheless, as I pursued lost relatives, certain resources sustained and comforted me. I offer them to you, dear reader, in the event that they may be of use.

BOOKS
Florence Fisher, *The Search for Anna Fisher*, Fawcett Crest, 1974
Betty Jean Lifton
  Lost and Found: The Adoption Experience, Harper Perennial, 1988
  Journey of the Adopted Self: A Quest for Wholeness, Basic Books, 1995
  Twice Born: Memoirs of an Adopted Daughter, St. Martin's, 1998

MOVIES
Secrets and Lies, Mike Leigh, Director, Twentieth Century Fox, 1996

SUPPORT ORGANIZATIONS AND NEWSLETTERS

NORCAP:

www.norcap.co.uk

A British charity, NORCAP helps people affected by adoption through an adoption register for searching adults, research and intermediary services, regional support groups, and a quarterly magazine, *NORCAP News*. NORCAP was established in 1982.

Adoptee-Birthparent Support Network:

www.adoptee-birthparentsupportnetwork.org

The Adoptee-Birthparent Support Network (ABSN) offers monthly support group meetings. ABSN is an all-volunteer search and support group serving people whose lives have been affected by adoption in Maryland, Virginia, Washington, DC, and related areas. ABSN is affiliated with the American Adoption Congress and is active in adoption reform efforts locally and nationally.

Metro Reunion Registry:

metroreunionregistry.org

The Metro Reunion Registry serves as a repository of information pertaining to adoption searches by all members of the adoption triad. Registrations include nearly every U.S. state, Canada, and over 20 foreign countries. Information is entered into the database upon receipt. In the event of a match with existing data, or a match with new incoming data, registrants are notified immediately.

International Soundex Reunion Registry (ISSR):

www.plumsite.com/isrr

ISSR is the world's largest free reunion registry dedicated to reuniting adult family members separated by adoption, divorce, or other dislocation. ISSR has reunited thousands of adults all over the world.

American Adoption Congress:

www.americanadoptioncongress.org

The American Adoption Congress represents those whose lives have been touched by adoption or other loss of family continuity. AAC comprises individuals, families and organizations committed to adoption reform.

Bastard Nation:

www.bastards.org

Bastard Nation advocates for the civil and human rights of adult citizens who were adopted as children. It campaigns on behalf of adopted adults to restore the right to their birth records. Currently, only five states in the United States of America allow adopted adults unrestricted access to their own original birth records.

Discussion Questions for Book Groups

1. How does the experience of adoption affect adopted people and their families? Is there a pattern or are the experiences uniquely personal? How were family relationships affected in *Swimming up the Sun*?

2. Sovereign countries treat adoption differently. The approach of the United Kingdom and the United States differ culturally and legally. Is one approach better than the other? What should be changed?

3. How could the social network have made the author's journey more straightforward?

4. Have open adoption and adoption reunions affected expectations and experiences of adoption? How?

5. What obligation, if any, do birth parents have toward their relinquished offspring? Likewise, what obligation do adopted people have to their birth parents and kin?

6. How would you have responded to the author's situation?

ORDER FORM

Swimming up the Sun: A Memoir of Adoption
by Nicole J. Burton

An adopted daughter of a Jewish father and an artist mother finds her place
in the world.

❑ YES, I want _____ signed copies of *Swimming up the Sun* at $14.95 each
   plus $4 shipping per book (Maryland residents please add $1.00 sales tax per book.)

   Shipping takes 3–5 business days.

   Canadian orders must be accompanied by a postal money order in U.S. funds; allow

   15 days for Canadian delivery.

   International orders: Add $10 for shipping per book. (U.K. buyers may purchase from
   Amazon.co.uk)

❑ My check or money order for $ _____ is enclosed.

Name _____

Organization _____

Address _____

City/State/Zip_____

Phone _____ Fax _____

E-mail_____

Please make your check payable to:
APC (Apippa Publishing Co.)
P.O. Box 54
Riverdale Park, MD 20738

To place a bulk order of 10 copies or more, e-mail Nicole@NicoleJBurton.com for
discount rates.

Guaranteed satisfaction or your money back

Printed in the United States
201722BV00001B/1-51/P

9 780979 89920